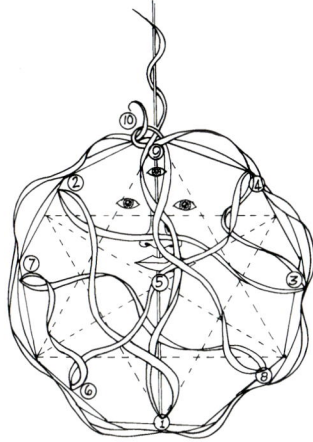

KATONAH YOGA
on the mat

NEVINE MICHAAN

KATONAH
YOGA®

katonahyoga.com   39 Main Street, Bedford Hills, NY 10507

Hand
the first a
D esires
hole
will to RISE
Rising through
Dawning of SPRING RISING
PASSAGE THROUGH TIME
ROUND of BEING
Descent into 1 the personal
RISK to SUBSTANTIATE
THE SOUL IN CONTAINMENT
AGE
ROOT of
ORGANIC NATUR
CIRCUMSTANCES.

The goal of this manual is to
inspire you to practice and play on the mat.

It is through practice that you become capable.
In a practice there are elements of self-responsibility,
personal motivation, and self-realization.

Yoga works.
The power of practice belongs to the individual.
It is powerful to measure up, to control your breath,
to be clear and well-directed.

It is joyful to be powerful, well-organized and well-oriented.

This manual is reflective of the yoga practiced
within the Katonah Yoga community.
The maps and meditations included are
specific to Katonah Yoga.

We encourage you
to use different techniques and overlay them.
Use your practice to your advantage.

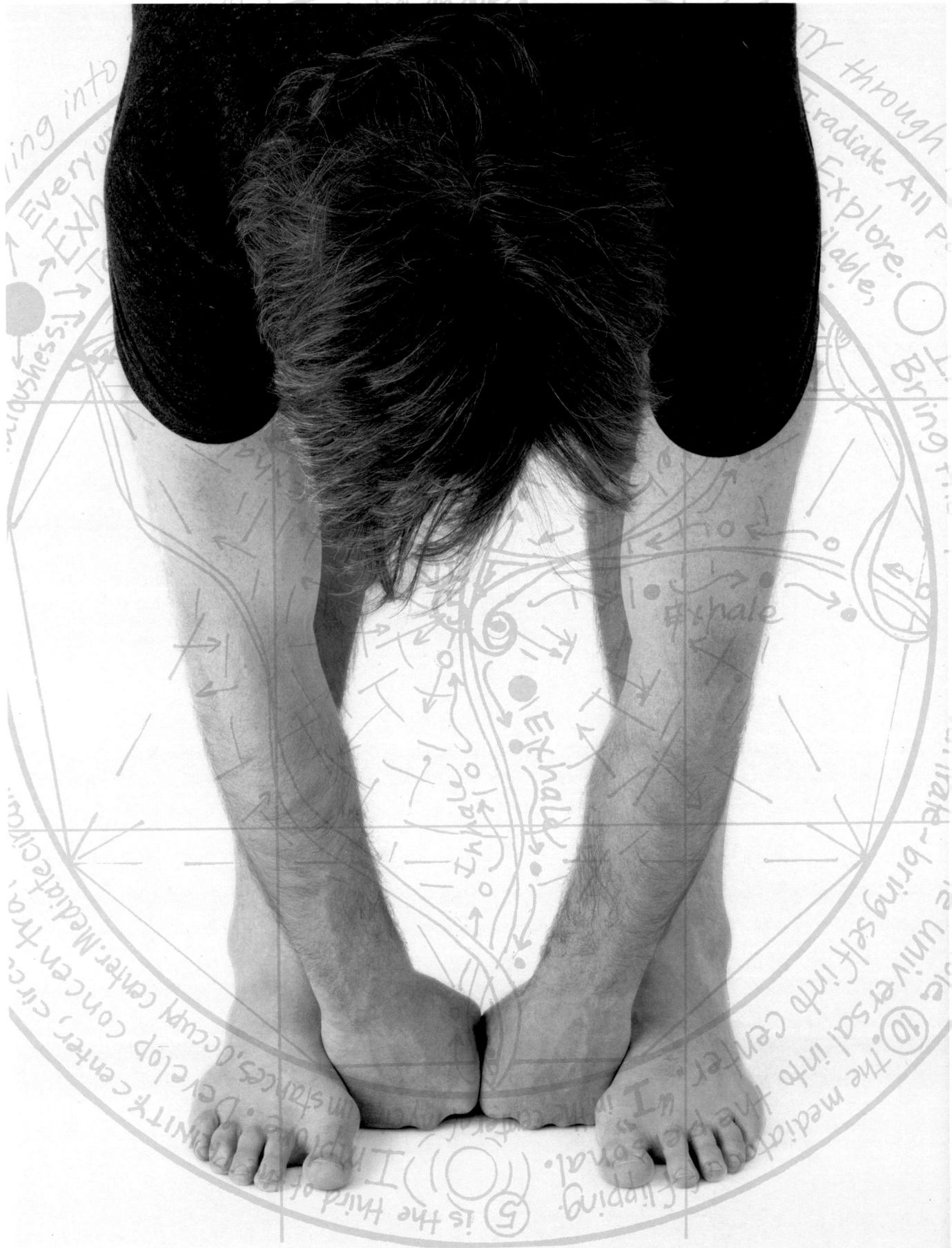

EXPANSIVE
SEEING
Uplifted
Framed
Boundaries
Fixed
Refine
Define
Eastern Light
FORMULATED VISION
TIME & SPACE
RISING
INNOCENCE
POTENTIAL
The FIRST
TRINITY
EAST
THYROID
STRENGTH
greater than the sum of its parts.

PROVIDENCE
DAWNING of FEELINGS
MOVEMENT INTO POTENTIAL
EFFORT of SPROUTING
FIRST SEX
PRODUCT of CONTACT
SPEECH
SEAT of the IMMUNE SYSTEM
Thymus Gland
Hand
left hand holding left hand nourishes the heart
heart
SPRING RISING
NATURE of FORM in the CONTAINER
ENTRY INTO FORM
Archetype in the BOX
ORGANIZED NATURE
CONTAINMENT
KIDNEYS
Ascension INTO WILLINGNESS
Descent into ORGANIC NATURE
FIRST GATE
UNDERSTANDING
GROWTH
EMBODIMENT
in its INTEGRITY

A hang is a standing forward fold.

It is superfunctional
for strengthening legs, stretching the spine
and taking pressure off your lower back,
neck and head.

The foundation is organized through the feet.
As you hang over, folding yourself in half, keep swaying
subtly back and forth on the feet.
Weight balanced in the balls of the feet
pitches you forward into the potential.
Weight in the heels makes the pose more static.
The goal is to sway across the arch of the foot, developing
a dynamic yet stationary posture.

Hangs are part of longevity practices—
the longer you stay with the pose, the easier it becomes
to rest and adjust your mind and breath.
Bend knees if you are tight, hang your torso
over your hips, and drop your head.

REVELATION

REFLECTION
GOAL SETTING
REACTION ②
VISION of
the DUSK

PEACE

⑨ MEDITATED VISION

POTENTIAL ④

VISION of
the DAWN

HANDLES
the WORLD
⑦
RIGHT

HANDLES
the HEART
③
LEFT

MOBILITY ⑥

VIRILITY

⑧ STABILITY
WILL POWER

PATIENCE

EFFORT
TENACITY

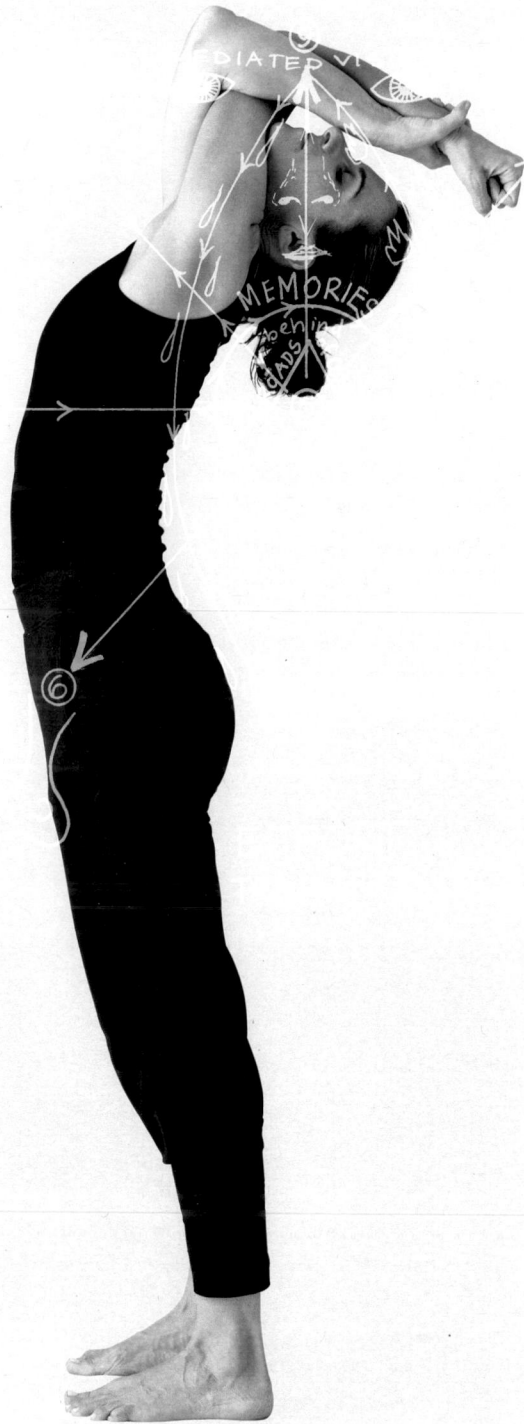

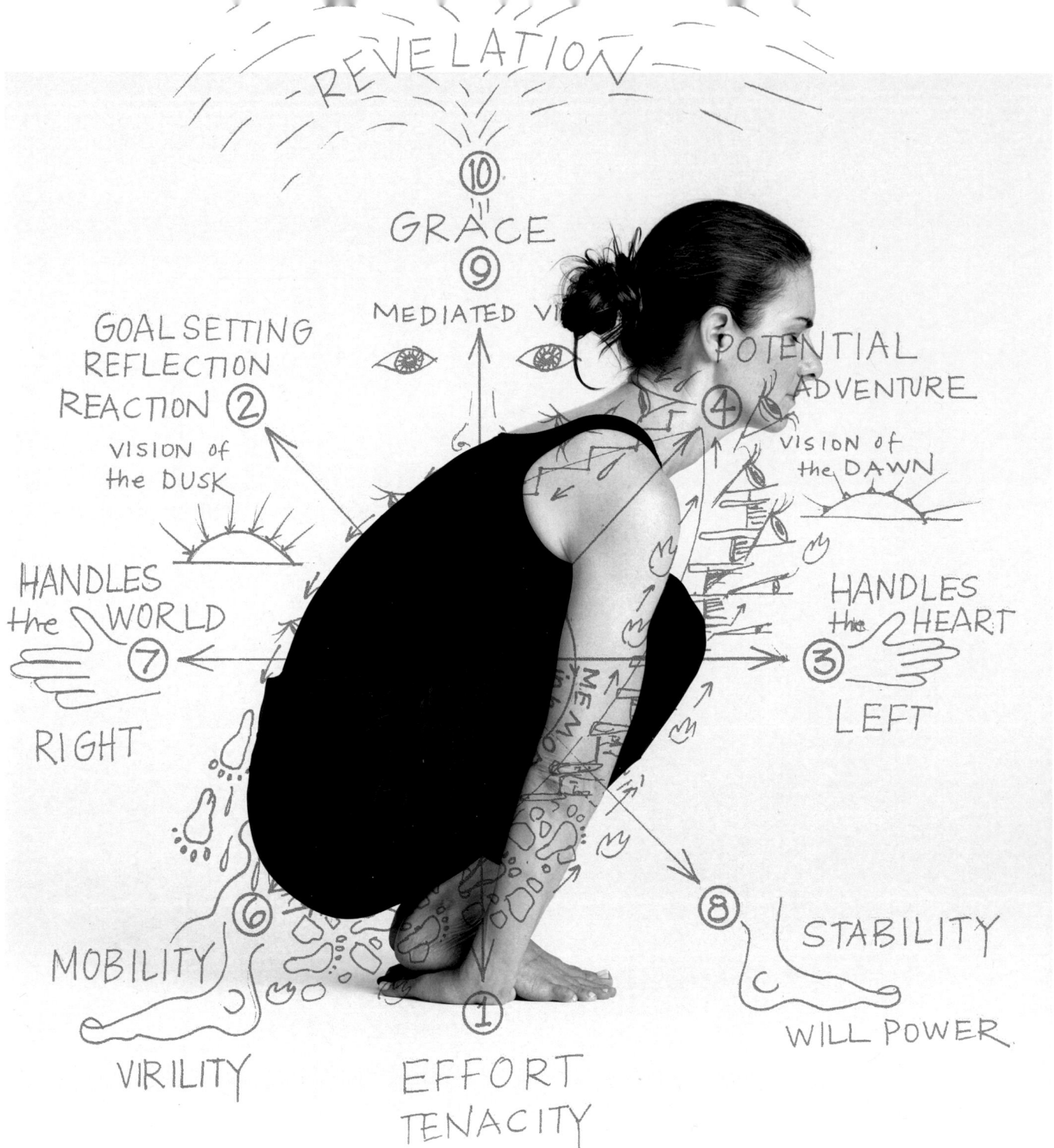

REVELATION

⑩
GRACE
⑨
MEDIATED VI...

GOAL SETTING
REFLECTION
REACTION ②

VISION of
the DUSK

POTENTIAL
ADVENTURE ④

VISION of
the DAWN

HANDLES
the WORLD
⑦

RIGHT

HANDLES
the HEART
③

LEFT

⑥
MOBILITY

①

⑧
STABILITY

WILL POWER

VIRILITY

EFFORT
TENACITY

REVELATION

⑩

GRACE

⑨

MEDIATED

GOAL SETTING
REFLECTION
REACTION ②

VISION of
the DUSK

POTENTIAL
ADVENTURE

VISION of
the DAWN

HANDLES
the WORLD
⑦

POTENTIAL
in front
ROADS

④

HANDLES
the HEART
③

RIGHT

LEFT

MOBILITY

⑥

⑧

STABILITY

VIRILITY

①

EFFORT
TENACITY

WILL POWER

DIRECTIONS to make ORIGAMI BOAT

①

Start with a square sheet of paper.

②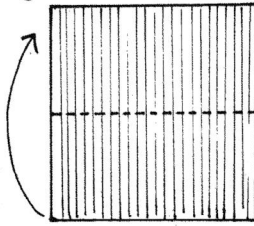

Fold in half along the midline.

③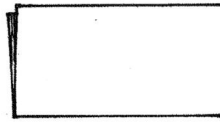

④

Fold in half again.

⑤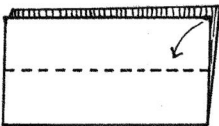

Then unfold halfway.

⑥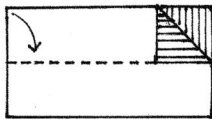

Fold corner down to the midline.

⑦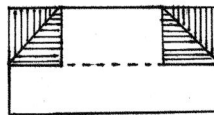

Fold other corner to the midline.

⑧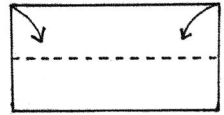

TURN PAPER OVER.

⑨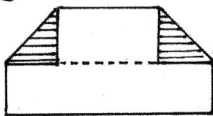

FOLD EACH CORNER DOWN TO THE MIDLINE.

⑩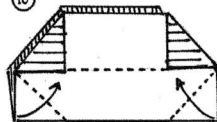

FOLD BOTTOM CORNER UP TO THE MIDLINE

⑪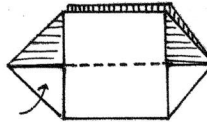

TURN OTHER CORNER UP TO THE MIDLINE

⑫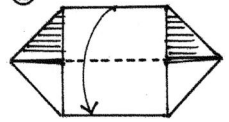

TAKE TOP HALF FRONT AND FOLD TO BOTTOM

⑬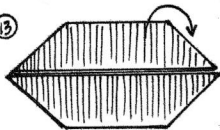

FOLD THE BACK HALF BACK BEHIND

⑭

CREASE AND THEN OPEN CENTER

⑮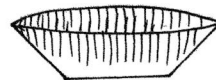

FORM BOAT.

You are designed to fit yourself. Your hands fit under your feet.
Good form ups function.
The magic is in the use of technique to measure up,
to get under yourself, to get over yourself, to get around yourself.

Asana is origami for bodies.

concentrating

•wellness•Willingness•   (right) Above (left)
occupy Center   ⑩ •Wholeness•   W ↕ E
Integrated   mediate polarities   Below
Reaction•Reflection•Memory   Embodiment   Rising the Vision in the Eastern Horizon   radiating
GOAL SETTING   WHOLE • ROUND • SPHERICAL •   VISION of POTENTIAL

VISION   ②   ④   PERCEIVING
                From WEST to EAST, From EXPERIENCE   Descent into meditation of the core
                                    ⑨

Hearing is vibratory   ROUND SOUND
ABILITY   ACOUSTICS
                                                                            Uplift
        Reflection   Center   INNOCENCE
        TR   of circum   Handling one's feelings
        Fulfill Obligations   ③
Handling the World   LEFT
                                        From WEST to EAST   Speech,
RIGHT   first articulation of feelings
                                                        Desires of the Heart
        •OCCUPY CENTER of one's CIRCUMSTANCES•   BOUYANT • HEALTHY • HAPPY • WISE •   DOING
        Through tenacity rise into capacity•
        Develop skills, handling the world   PASSAGE THROUGH TIME
        VISION in the root of the world   techniques to facilitate descent into age   RISING of WILL: WILL RISE

STABILITY   ⑥   ⑧   BEING
        RISK to SUBSTANTIATE   GROUND   AGE
                SEX   Descent into ① the personal   ROOT of
        Establishing one's footing   ORGANIC NATURE
                in the WORLD   THE SOUL IN CONTAINMENT   Substantiated in Time

        PATERNAL ROOT   DEPTH of EMBODIMENT   MATERNAL ROOT

KATONAH YOGA © 2014   by Nevine Michaan © 2014

concentrating

Reaction· Reflection· Memory

GOAL SETTING ②

·wellness· Willingness· occupy center Integrated

WHOLE · ROUND · SPHERICAL

(right) Above (left)
W ← → E

⑩ ·Wholeness· mediate polarities Embodiment
Below

radiating

Rising the Vision in the Eastern Horizon
VISION of POTENTIAL ④

VISION

PERCEIVING

From WEST to EAST. From EXPERIENCE TO...

⑨

Descent into meditation of the...

Hearing is vibratory

ABILITY

Reflection TRUST Fulfill O...
the World

Handling
RIGHT

⑦

rise into capacity, handling the world
Through tenacity
Develop skills,

·OCCUPY CENTER of one's CIRCUMSTANCES·

STABILITY

mediator

Center circumference

VIBRATION

DESCENT into EAST

Half

Development of...

Ascending

GROUND of BEING

Descent into ① the person

THE SOUL IN CONTAINMENT

RISK to SUBSTANTIATE
SEX
Establishing one's footing
in the WORLD

PATERNAL ROOT

⑥

DEPTH of EMBODIMENT

ROUND SOUND
ACOUSTICS

Uplift

INNOCENCE

Handling one's feelings
LEFT

of feelings
the Heart

DOING

·BOUYANT· HEALTHY· HAPPY· WISE·

Deriving will
SPRING RISE

techniques to facilitate descent into age

PASSING THROUGH TIME

⑧

BEING

AGE
ROOT of
ORGANIC NATURE
Substantiated in Time·

MATERNAL ROOT

KATONAH YOGA © 2014

by Nevine Michaan © 2014

TRACE OF A STEP.

TIPTO

STAND.

FLEXING

Earth Contact

Earthe Vision

of Insight

Epitome

Awakened

Personal inheritance

Umbilical Cord

The Tenacity of

descending down from the Universe

CHARACTER OF
VIRILITY ⑥
MALE ROOT
TAKING A RISK
ADVENTURE·
STOCK·

earth, metal, water, wood)
STIR· Integration of
ED 23's or 32's
LOVE △ · ▽

WEST
EAST
WESTWEST EAST EAST

Ⓔ

⑥

BOTTOM
POTENTIAL
SOLE

⑨

④ FUTURE
PUMP
ACCELERATOR
moves into potential

BRIDGE
⑤
③ ARCH ⑦ west
MEDIATION
PRESENT
ALERTNESS

Vesica Piscis

POSITIONS
YOU IN
the
⑧ PAST ⑥
HEEL
①

STABILITY Bones

Soul Embodi

FIRE SUBSTANTIATING

First Gate

Planted on EARTH

eliminating

Primal Insight

Depth of Insight

TRINITY OF GROUND

PORTAL TIM

PLACE

STABILITY

ON EARTH

①

WILL POWER·
MATERNAL
ROOT· FOOT
OF HOME
· KNOWLEDGE
FORM· P
embodimen
· LEFT ROOT ⑧
substantia
ORGANIZED NA

Achilles Heel

Age

EAST
EASTEAST? WEST

Ⓦ

the Ar
th

Reproductive

brakes

⑥

BOTTOM
POTEN
SO

⑨

LUNGS

KIDNEYS
ARCH
of ADRENALS

⑤ ③

west

REPRODUCTIVE

⑥ ⑧

①

LEFT BOTTOM

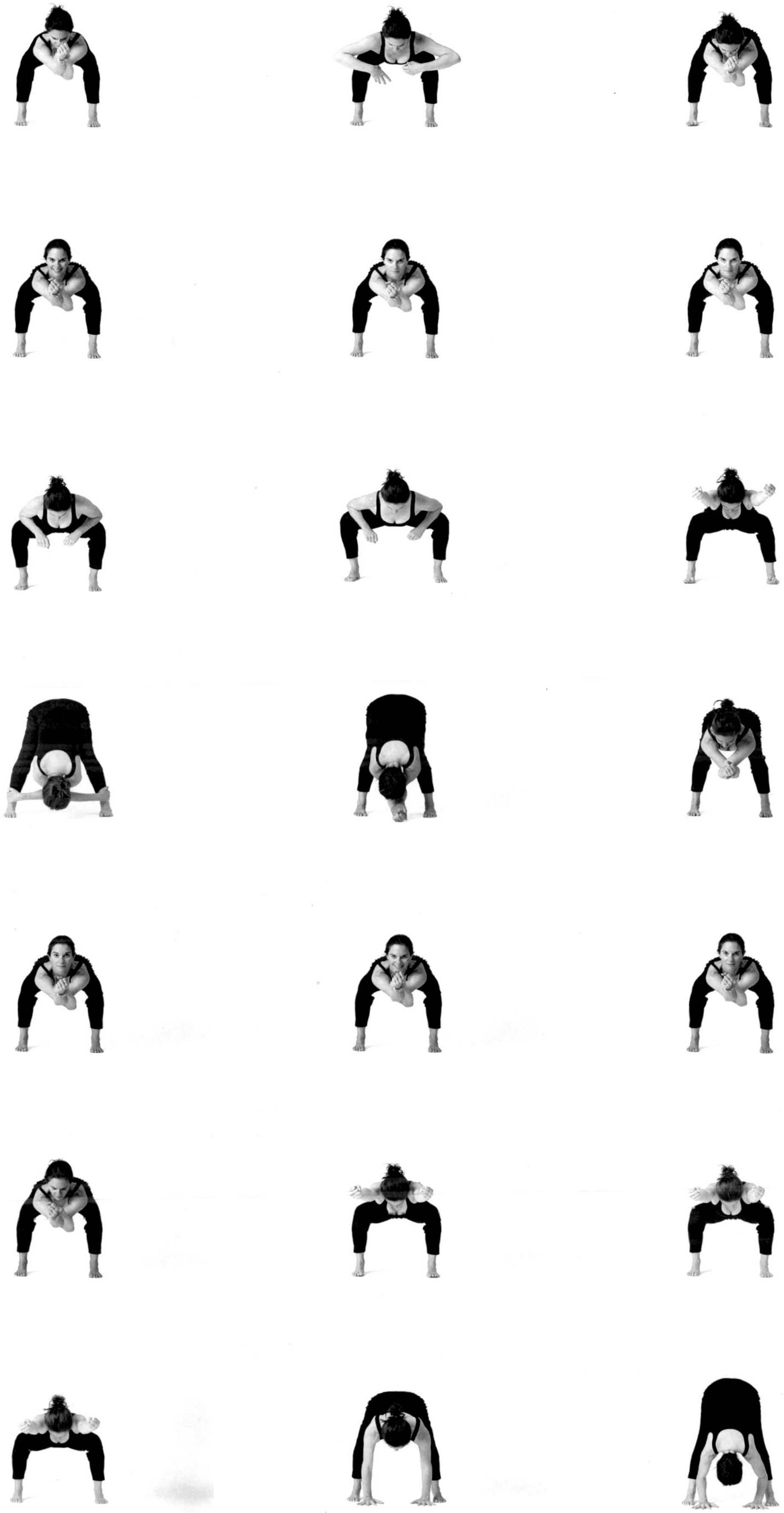

REVELATION
⑩

GRACE
⑨

GOAL SETTING
REFLECTION
REACTION ②

VISION of
the DUSK

MEDIATED VISION

POTENTIAL
④ VISION of
the DAWN

HANDLES
the WORLD
⑦
RIGHT

HANDLES the
HEART ③
LEFT

MOBILITY
VIRILITY ⑥

⑧ STABILITY
WILL POWER

PATIENCE

①
EFFORT
TENACITY

GRACE

9

MEDIATED VISION

GOALSETTING
REFLECTION
REACTION

2

POTENTIA

4

VISION of
the DAWN

VISION of
the D SK

HANDLES
the WORLD

7

RIGHT

HAND
the

3

LEF

MEMORIES
behind
consciousness
ROADS
5
POTENTIAL
cross roads

MOBILIT

VIRILITY

1

EFFORT
TENACITY

STAB

WILL POW
PATIEN

Breath, prana, holds the chemistry of the universe; the ions, the ores, the minerals that surround us and inform us. It is the space dust of grace reigning through our atmosphere.

Breathing is a process of eating, feeding the mind and imagination as well as the body. A trained breath stabilizes the nervous system and communicates with deeper parts of oneself as well as ones surroundings.

A character of the breath is movement. A character of the mind is directing, channeling the momentum.

Great Nature's breaths move the great currents; the movement of the tides, the currents of wind, the planetary rotations. The breath of plants, insects, seasons, the breaths of fire and water belong to the breaths of our planet. It is the breath that enlivens. Great Nature supports the individual breath and builds the momentum on the collective breath. The great movements of breath are very soulful and spirited.

All our meditations are based on integrating the personal breath with the breaths of Great Nature using the Golden Thread of a skilled imagination.

KATONAH YOGA BREATHWORK

Breathwork is the magic of yoga. It enlivens the mind and body.

The power of postures and meditation is the breath.

Empower your well-being through breath practices.

The body is the instrument,
the mind is the musician,
and the breath is the melody.

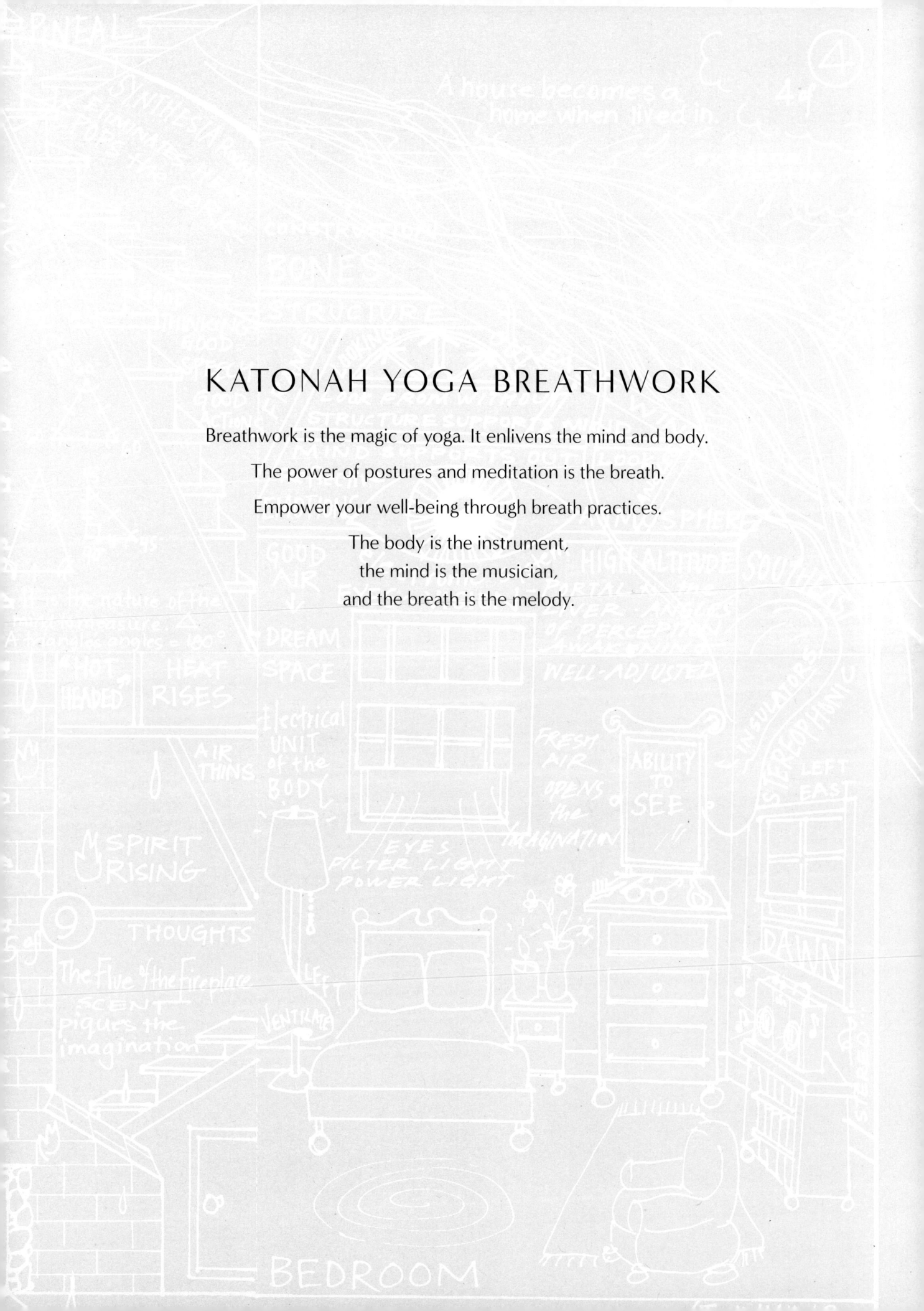

TRAVELING KAPALABHATI THROUGH THE MAGIC SQUARE

From a Katonah Yoga Teacher Training Class, 2019 with Nevine Michaan

Kapalabhati breath belongs to a series of fire breaths. The emphasis is on quick, forceful short breaths.
The muscles of the stomach and diaphragm are pumped to push the breath out the nostrils.
This breath helps regulate your internal temperature, enlivening your body and mind.
Traveling through the circuitry of the staircase, strengthens personal neurology.
Position yourself, be formal but comfortable. Orient yourself; mouth closed, tongue on palette,
hearing connecting to breathing. Guide yourself in an oceanic breath, pulled and filtered through your
throat. Bring your arms up, turn your palms up.

If you know your kapalabhati breathing, if you know your Magic Square, the art of this technique is you're going to count to 100, directing the breath through a neurological circuit. The first 10 kapalabhatis, you want to travel down to room 1. The second 10 kapalabhatis, you're going to travel to room 2, which is the right hand up in the air. The third 10, which will get you to 30, will bring you around the heart. The fourth will bring you to the left hand held above you. Fifth will bring you to the middle. Sixth will bring you to the right leg. Seventh will bring you to the right armpit. Eighth will bring you to the left leg. Ninth will bring you to the third eye. And tenth will put it together.

We're going to do kapalabhati to 100 counts and your job is to follow the steps and descend the ladders, ascend the ladders, and do it all skipping through kapalabhati. If you can do 100 and you're fine then I'm going to take you backwards and do it 99, 98, 97... so that you can unravel the knot. So when you do it 1, 2, 3, 4, 5, 6, 7, 8, 9, you're going to build a Celtic knot. When you do it 9, 8, 7, 6, 5, 4, 3, 2, 1, you're going to unravel the knot. In life, you have you know how to put it together and you have to know how to take it apart.

Connect your hearing to your breathing. Remember that hearing always puts you in the dialogue of kidneys: hearing the alarms, making sure that you're safe in the center of your circumference. Breathing brings you in the dialogue of competency, the lungs. When you connect your hearing to your breathing, you connect your competency to your stability, your ability to your stability.

When you're ready, take a nice deep breath in. Exhale completely and then start to count. So it's out, out, out, out, out, out, out, out, out. 10, 11, 12, 13, 14, 15, 16, 17, 18, 19, 20, 21, 22, 23, 24, 25, 26, 27, 28, 29, 30, 1, 2, 3, 4, 5, 6, 7, 8, 9, 40, 41, 42, 43, 44, 45, 46, 47, 48, 49, 50, 1, 2, 3, 4, 5, 6, 7, 8, 9, 60, 61, 62, 63, 64, 65, 66, 67, 68, 69, 70, 71, 2, 3, 4, 5, 6, 7, 8, 9, 80, 81, 2, 3, 4, 5, 6, 7, 8, 9, 90. Pop it through. 91, 2, 3, 4, 5, 6, 7, 8, 9, 100.

Take a nice a deep breath. Hold your breath then exhale nice and easy. Keep your arms up if you can and now, again, nice deep breath. You're starting from above. Exhale. Inhale again. And then, when you're ready, we're going to go from 100 down. 99, 98, 97, 96, 95, 94, 93, 92, 91, 90, 89, 88, 87, 86, 85, 84, 83, 82, 81, 80, 79, 78, 77, 76, 75, 74, 73, 72, 71, 70, 69, 68, 67, 66, 65, 64, 63, 62, 61, 60, 59, 58, 57, 56, 55, 54, 53, 52, 51, 50, 49, 48, 47, 46, 45, 44, 43, 42, 41, 40, 39, 38, 37, 36, 35, 34, 33, 32, 31, 30, 29, 28, 27, 26, 25, 24, 23, 22, 21, 20, 19, 18, 17, 16, 15, 14, 13, 12, 11, 10, 9, 8, 7, 6, 5, 4, 3, 2, 1.

TRAVELING THE MASTER STAIRCASE

Take a deep breath. Hold it with a pregnant pause. If comfortable, take three more quick inhalations. Hold your breath, building heat and attention. When you are ready to exhale, use your imagination and direct your breath out through the top of your head; popping the cork, letting the genie out of the bottle. Descend your arms, allow the grace to descend.

As you inhale , let your fires rise.
As you exhale , let your waters descend.
As you inhale, make your efforts.
As you exhale, be graceful.

TRINITY
SUMMER
CENTER of CIRCUMFERENCE
The Crossroads of Consciousness
Reflective of the Whole
5
RADIATING
CONCENTRATING
VIBRATION of WELL-BEING
SOUTH of ONE'S
HEART
CONSCIOUSNESS INTO the PERSONAL
FORM
The SEED
The WHOLE
PLUMB LINE
EFFORT
•FIRE•
•WATER•
INSIGHT
•EARTH•
MATERNAL ROOT
Endocrine
GRACE
FIRST GATE

SCRIPT OF A BREATHING CLASS, 2021

By virtue of connecting with your breath, the goal of this practice is to strengthen your lungs, soothe your nerves and nourish your imagination.

Begin from wherever you are by organizing yourself. Image yourself in the middle of a sphere. Close your mouth gently, touching the tip of your tongue to the roof of your palette.

Breathe through your nose, smelling the air and pulling the breath in to the throat. Connect yourself to the sound and movement of your breath. Encourage your breath to be oceanic; moving a rhythmic inhalation and exhalation. The inhalation holds the tide moving in, the exhalation, the tide moving out. Carry the breath through the doors of the nostrils. Hear the breath through the portals of the ears. The oceanic breath soothes the nerves, it is rhythmic and fulfilling. The tide moves in, the tide moves out, and then the tide moves in again.

Fill yourself up, empty yourself out; the oceanic breath connects your breath to one of the great breaths of the planet. Inhale as the tide moves in, exhale as the tide moves out.

A second breathing technique is organized around the nature of fire to ascend and water to descend. Fire holds the character of effort and vigilance. Water holds the character of grace and fluency. In this technique the rising of fire is imaged with the inhalation rising up your back, and the exhalation, imaged as rain falling down in front of you, guided by the mind to see the potential. A circuit of breathing in and out, up and down, front and back.

So let's try again, put yourself in the middle of yourself, put the tip of the tongue lightly on the upper palette, keep the hearing connected to the breathing, and this time, guided by the imagination, as you inhale, image fire is rising up behind you, and as you exhale image water is raining down in front of you.

As you inhale and fire rises, the characters of fire are those of attention, vigilance, action. And as you exhale, the characters of water holds grace and fluency and direction. We imagine the inhalation rising behind you, reflecting memory. And we make the exhalation descend down in front of you allowing grace to be in the potential. You inhale up the back, and you can

exhale down the front. A nice way to complete this breath, is to take the breath up the center imagining you have fire underneath water which allows you to build up temperature so you can use the inhalation as steam rising up the center of yourself and then you can pop the cork and you can rain out in to your circumference.

Move your breath through this circuit several times. Inhaling up the back, exhaling down the front, inhaling is fire rising, exhaling is water descending and then inhaling as steam rises through the center and then rising popping through yourself, exhaling to allow the grace to descend around you.

When you get tired, rest in your natural breath.

The next technique, the breath of the seasons, adds the defining moments of the held breath and the empty breath.

A breath naturally has 4 parts: an in breath, a hold with a pregnant pause, an out breath, and a hold with an empty pause.

The oceanic breath soothes and strengthens the nerves with its rhythmic balance. The breath of fire and water moves the circuitry of temperature. This breath is imaged as surrounding you.

The breath of the seasons connects you with the rhythm of the year. When you inhale, image spring is rising in front and around you, the sprouting of nature. As you hold your breath, full and overhead, image summer is ripening, the held breath is like ripening fruit above you.

When you exhale, image autumn leaves falling behind you and around you so memories descend, With the empty breath image winter in the depths beneath you and then, again, inhale let spring rise. Be revolutionary with this breath circuit. As you inhale spring is potentiating, as you hold your breath summer is ripening, as you're exhaling autumn is reflecting and as you're empty you get those moments of insights in winter, knowing that spring rises again.

The breath can be autonomic, moving by itself, and it can be sympathetic, it can be manipulated. You can move the breath as the ocean, allowing the tide to move in, the tide to move out and filling yourself up

with that oceanic nature, with that character that is inherent in our planet. You can manipulate your breath, playing with temperature rising up in your inhalation and building heat and then descending on your exhalation, manipulating water and cooling things down. And then you play with your seasons, surrounding yourself with the inhalation, spring rising, holding your breath, summer ripening, exhaling descending memories, and being empty getting the insights of winter. And then inhaling again.

Let your breath be natural again.

We have one more technique in this practice. It is a breath of measure, it is a technique to build stamina, to build lung capacity. In this breath we are going to take a full breath and we are going to break it down into four parts. This practice really teaches you to measure up.

One can imagine dividing a breath in four equal parts, together adding up to one full breath. Inhale, inhale, inhale, inhale, pause, and once you are nice and full you take an exhalation through the top of your head like smoke rising up through a chimney to let it all out.

So it's going to be four parts on the in breath and one part on the out breath.

Take a nice deep breath inhaling and exhaling completely.

Each inhale takes in the same quantity of breath, like measuring a full cup by measuring quarter cups. So it is four parts in and one part out. Inhale, inhale, inhale, inhale, hold it for a moment and then one smooth exhale. And again inhale, inhale, inhale, inhale, hold and then exhale. Beautiful, one last time, inhale, inhale, inhale, inhale, hold and then let it all out.

Now let's try the opposite. So this time you're going to take a full breath in and we're going to let it out in four parts. Exhale, exhale, exhale, exhale, pause and then take a nice long inhalation and fill it all up. Then exhale, exhale, exhale, exhale and then hold it for a moment and take a long inhalation and then again exhale, exhale, exhale, exhale and take a long inhalation.

And now just breath evenly. Take it in and out, let yourself be full, be empty, keep yourself attentive by using your mind, using your form, using your breath. Just keep filling yourself up and emptying yourself out.

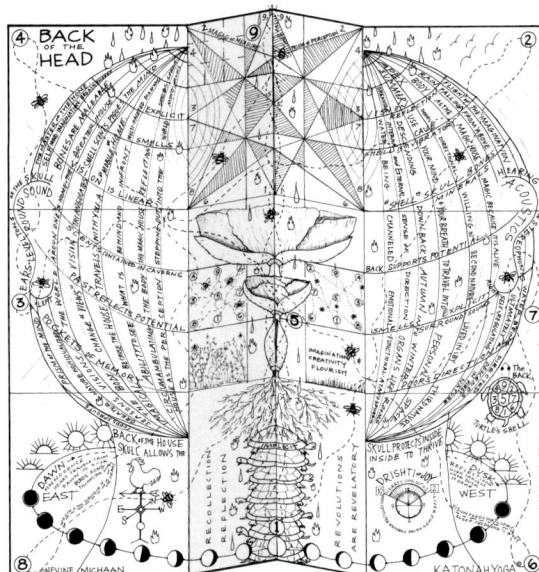

We are going to take the breath we just did and we are going to put it all together, three times, break the breath down into four parts on the inhale and four parts on the exhale.

As I said, this is a breath of measure. It builds volume, it builds control, it allows you to become very familiar with the fact that you can move your breath and direct your breath.

When you are ready take a deep breath in, exhale completely and we'll do four parts in and four parts out. So when you're ready it is inhale, inhale, inhale, inhale, hold it for a second and then exhale, exhale, exhale, exhale, hold it for a moment and then inhale, inhale, inhale, inhale then hold it for a moment and exhale exhale, exhale, exhale. One last time, inhale, inhale, inhale, inhale and then exhale, exhale, exhale, exhale.

Then take one long inhalation, fill yourself up and when you're ready just take it nice and easy and exhale through the top of the head, knowing that is your chimney and it is really the best place to let all the heat out.

Rest in your natural breath

We have done four breathing techniques; breath of the ocean, breath of fire and water, breath of the seasons, and a breath for measure and volume. These breaths are surrounding and intimate. Breathing techniques build lung capacity. Breathing techniques empower your mind and body.

OPENING SEQUENCE

This practice is designed to adjust
the major glands of your endocrine system.
Set a breath count and be consistent.
Pick a number count. A count of 100
allows one to travel through
the circuitry of numbers.

4. Make yourself available

3. Connect to the Greater Whole

2. Clear the mind

1. Frame the vision

OPENING SEQUENCE

Four postures to open yourself up to your surroundings.

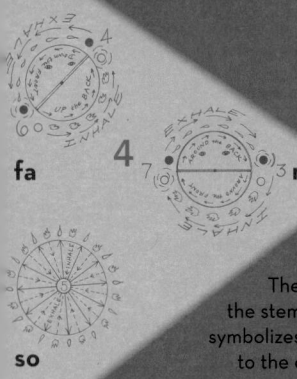

OCTAVE ABOVE

fa 4 7 **mi**

so

Meditation

re

The Tai Chi—
the stem of the cherry
symbolizes our connection
to the octave above

The grace
of the greater whole.
All the glands work
together for personal
harmony.

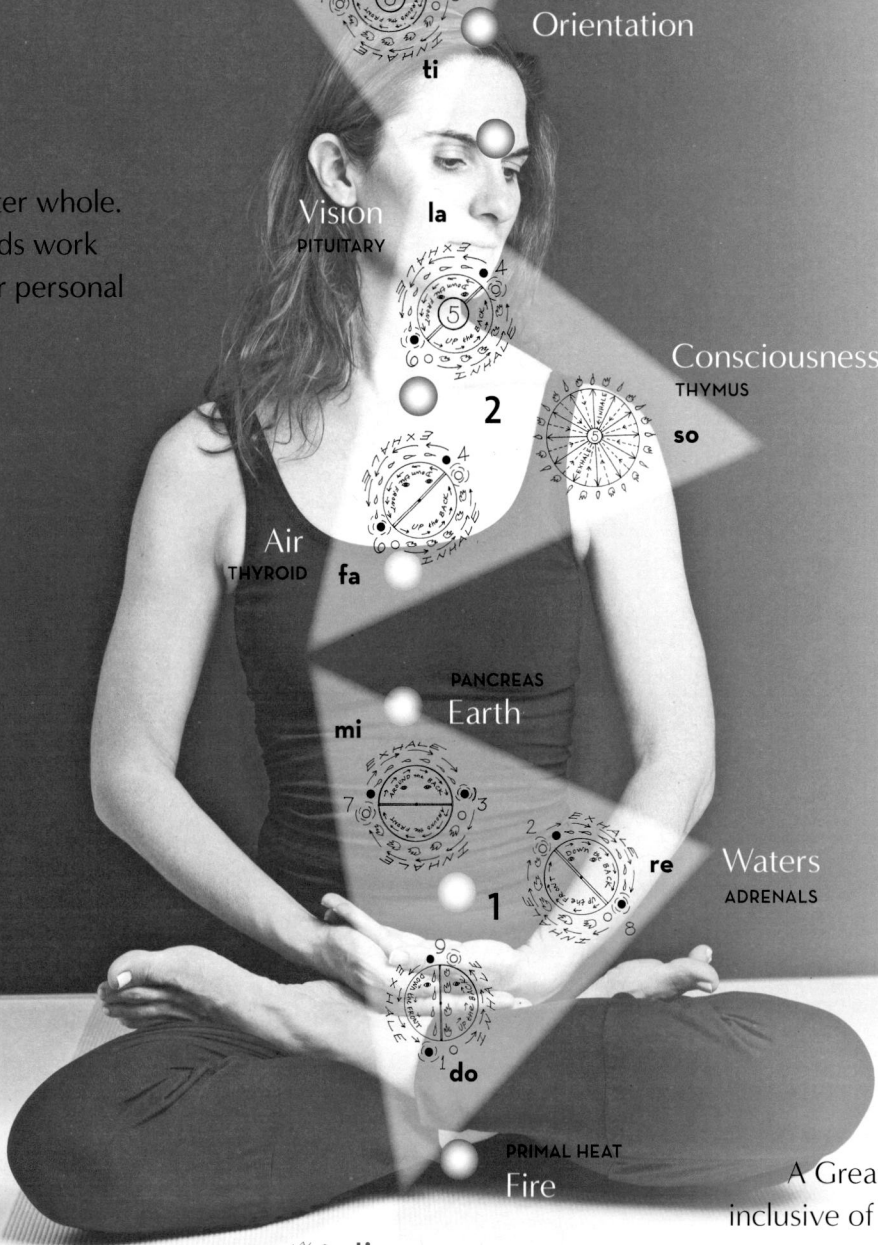

do Integration
THE ENDOCRINE SYSTEM

3

PINEAL
ti Orientation

Vision
la
PITUITARY

Consciousness
THYMUS
2 **so**

Air
THYROID **fa**

PANCREAS
mi Earth

Waters
re ADRENALS
1

do

PRIMAL HEAT
Fire

A Great Round
inclusive of 3 octaves—
7 steps, 21 notes.

OCTAVE BELOW

fa

so 7

ti

la

Grace

Meditation
HIGHER OCTAVE
re

Integration
INTEGRATED OCTAVE
do

Orientation
PINEAL
ti

Dawn & Dusk
PITUITARY
la

Finding Center
THYMUS
so

Parting the Waves
THYROID
fa

Watching your Back
PANCREAS
mi

Stiring the Pot
ADRENALS
re

Cats & Cows
PRIMAL FIRE
do

REVELATION

Meditation

re

Integration

do

ti

la

so

fa

mi

re

do

This practice starts at the bottom and goes up through the sequence of glands. Each technique uses the mind to direct the movement, intention and breath. Each breath is counted.

. **Do**— Cats and Cows: *Generates heat, stokes the primal flame of personal embodiment*

2. **Re**— Stiring the Pot *moves water, balances kidneys and equilibrium.*

3. **Me**— Watching your Back *pumps the diaphram using a bellows breath to support muscles and digestion.*

4. **Fa**— Parting the Waves *opens the lungs, builds strength and stamina. Supports the thyroid.*

5. **So**— Finding Center, Mediating Circumference, *making contact with oneself using a rhythmic out-breath. Strengthens the thymus gland.*

6. **La**— Dawn and Dusk, *inhaling to the left, exhaling to the right, traversing the arc of potential. Flushes the liver, supports vision and reflection engages the pituitary.*

7. **Ti**— Orientation *stimulates the pineal gland, supporting alertness, orientation.*

8. **Do**— Integration *stokes the imagination, builds internal pressure. Complete with a sustained pregnant pause before final liberating exhalation.*

9. **Re**— Meditation, *sitting in a harmonious state of being; well oriented, well organized, well adjusted.*

43

concentrating

Reaction. Reflection. Memory
GOAL SETTING
②

wellness. Willingness.
occupy center
Integrated
WHOLE · ROUND · SPHERICAL ·

⑩ Wholeness.
mediate polarities. Below
Embodiment

Rising the Vision in the Eastern Horizon
VISION of POTENTIAL

(right) Above (left)
W ←→ E

radiating

VISION

ABILITY

Hearing is vibratory

Reflection
TRUST
Fulfill Obligations

Handling the World

RIGHT

⑦
From

into capacity

OCCUPY CENTER of one's CIRCUMSTANCE

⑨

Descent into your world

④

ACOUSTICS

ROUND SOUND

UPLIFT

INNOCENCE

③

Handling one's feelings

LEFT

Speech,
the first articulation of feelings

Desires of the Heart

PERCEIVING

DOING

BEING

Half of the Whole

Development of experiences

techniques to facilitate descent

PASSAGE THROUGH TIME

Descent into your world

STABILITY

RISK to SUBSTANTIATE
SEX
Establishing one's footing
in the WORLD

PATERNAL ROOT

GROUND of BEING
① the personal

THE SOUL IN CONTAINMENT

DEPTH of EMBODIMENT

AGE
ROOT of
ORGANIC NATURE
Substantiated in Time

MATERNAL ROOT

⑧

concentrating

radiating

•Wellness•Willingness•
•occupy center•
Integrated
ROUND•SPHERICAL•

(right) Above (left)
W ←→ E

Wholeness
mediate polarities•Below
Embodiment

Reaction•Reflection•Memory
GOAL SETTING

Rising the Vision in the Eastern Horizon
VISION OF POTENTIAL

WHOLE

VISION

PERCEIVING

Hearing is vibratory

Acoustics

ROUND SOUND

ABILITY

Reflection
TRUST
Fulfill Obligations

INNOCENCE

Handling
the World

Center of
circumference

throbbing in the HEART

feelings

RIGHT

LEFT

Speech,
the first articulation of feelings
Desires of the Heart

DOING•ACTING

OCCUPY CENTER of ONE'S CIRCUMSTANCE

from WEST to EAST

Half of the Whole

Development of experiences

BOUYANT•HEALTHY•HAPPY•WISE

STABILITY

BEING

PASSAGE THROUGH TIME

GROUND of BEING
Descent into ① the personal

RISK to SUBSTANTIATE
SEX
Establishing one's footing
in the WORLD

THE SOUL IN CONTAINMENT

AGE
ROOT of
ORGANIC NATURE
Substantiated in Time

PATERNAL ROOT

DEPTH OF EMBODIMENT

MATERNAL ROOT

by Nevine Michaan © 2014

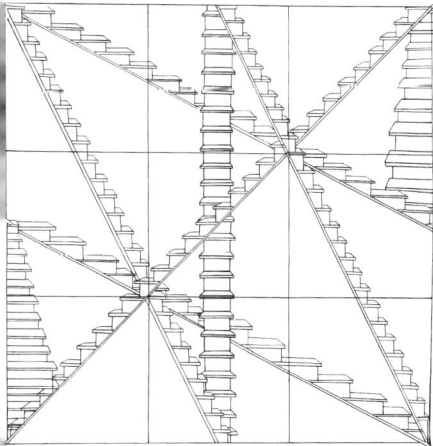 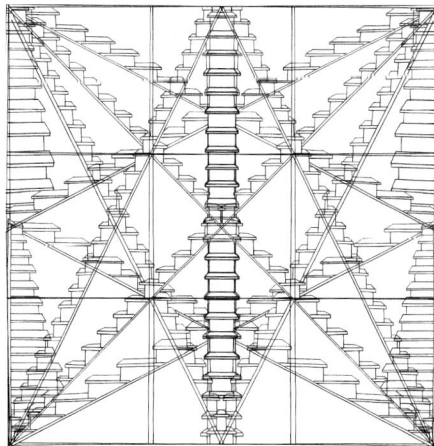 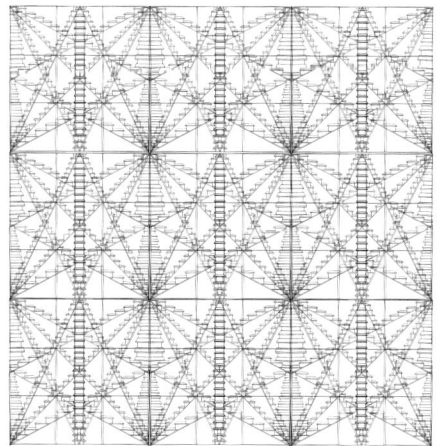

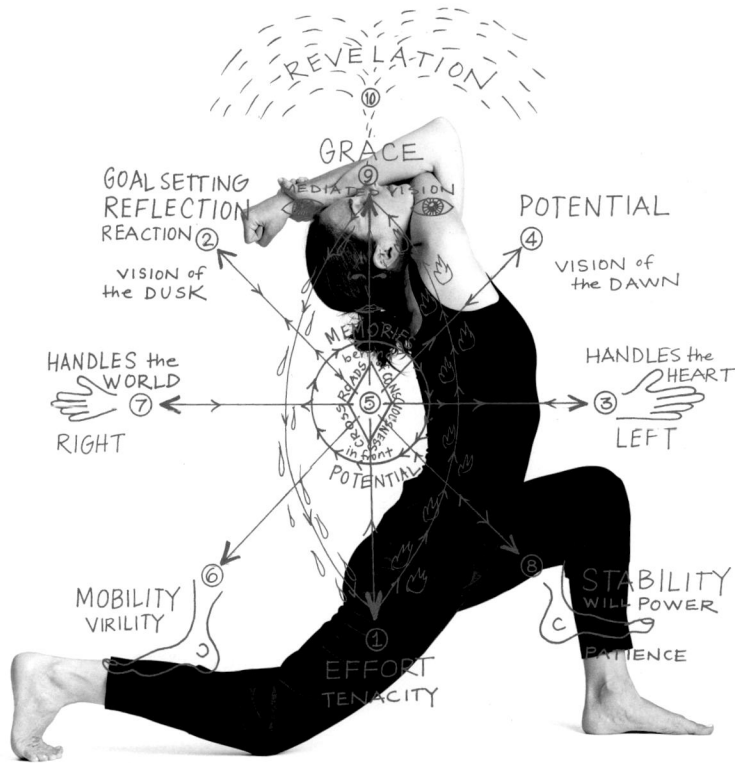

REVELATION
①

GRACE
⑨

MEDIATED VISION

GOALSETTING
REFLECTION
REACTION
②

POTENTIAL
④
VISION of
the DAWN

VISION of
the DUSK

HANDLES
the WORLD
⑦

RIGHT

MEMORIES

POTENTIAL
CROSSROADS
of CONSCIOUSNESS
front

HANDLES
the HEART
③

LEFT

MOBILITY
⑥

VIRILITY

EFFORT
TENACITY
①

STABILITY
⑧

WILL POWER
PATIENCE

REVELATION

GOAL SETTING
REACTION ②
REFLECTION
VISION OF
the DUSK

MEDIATED VISION

⑩

⑨

POTENTIAL
VISION OF
the DAWN

④

HANDLES
the WORLD ⑦

RIGHT

HANDLES
the HEART ③

LEFT

VIRILITY

STABILITY
WILL POWER

EFFORT
TENACITY

PATIENCE

Techniques work, they build skill.
The magic of great techniques is they demand time and measure
and presence until they become effortless.

Becoming literate is joyful.
Using ones literacy is transformative.

Fluency is no different in yoga
than any other skill. There needs to be a desire
or necessity to learn a language.
The time learning to conjugate verbs, learn vocabulary
and sentence structure, metaphor, idioms is tedious,
confusing and defeating.
Love drives a lot. If you have a wonderful experience,
the desire becomes strong enough.

Once you own a proficiency in a learnt language, things change.
It is no longer about the learning, but the using...
the joy of communicating comfortably and
effervescently in a second language.

It helps to have good teachers.
But if the desire is strong enough
one finds a way to learn.

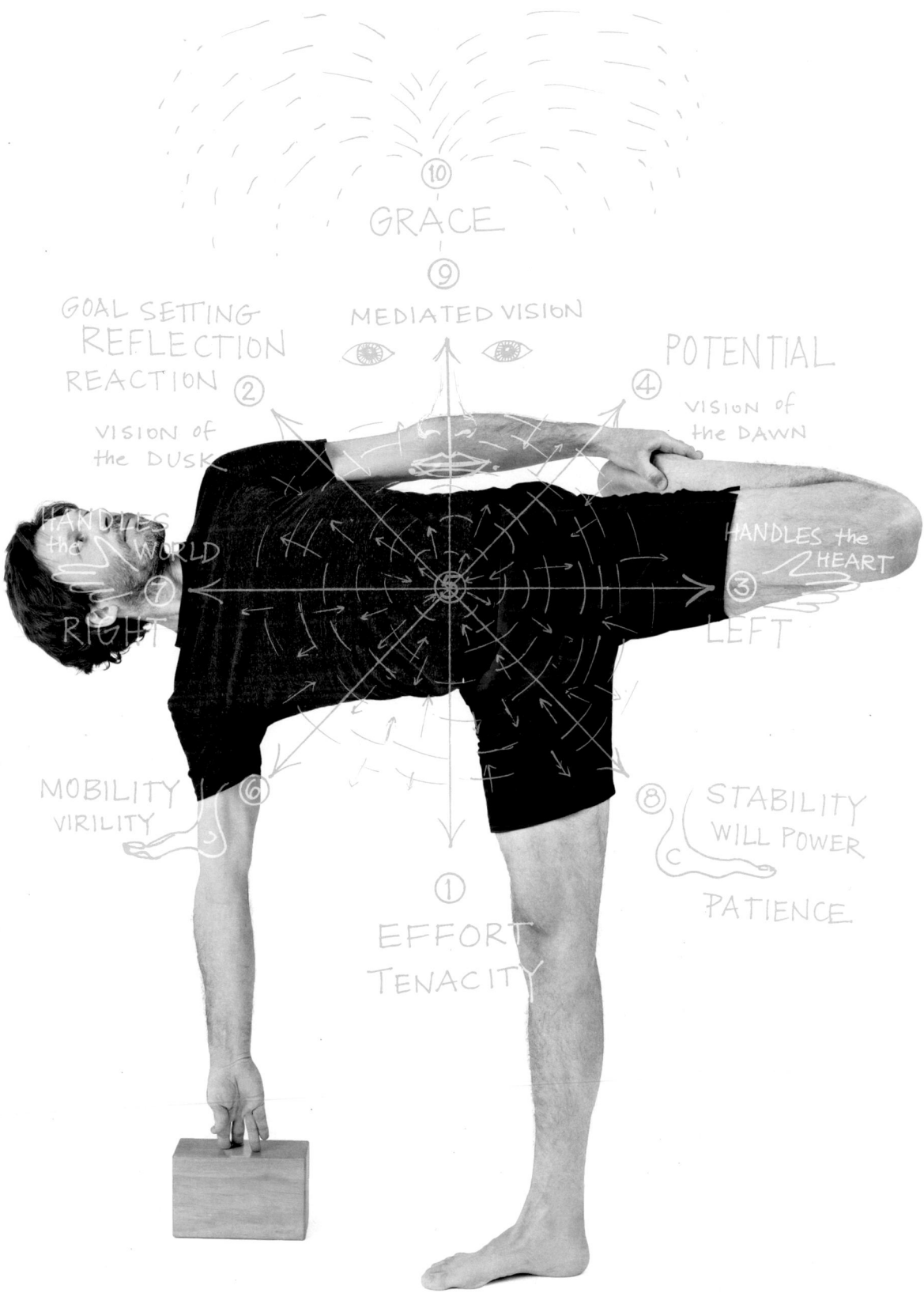

GRACE
⑩

⑨
MEDIATED VISION

GOAL SETTING
REFLECTION
REACTION ②

VISION of
the DUSK

POTENTIAL
④
VISION of
the DAWN

HANDLES
the WORLD
①
RIGHT

⑤

HANDLES the
HEART
③
LEFT

MOBILITY
VIRILITY ⑥

⑧
STABILITY
WILL POWER

PATIENCE

①
EFFORT
TENACITY

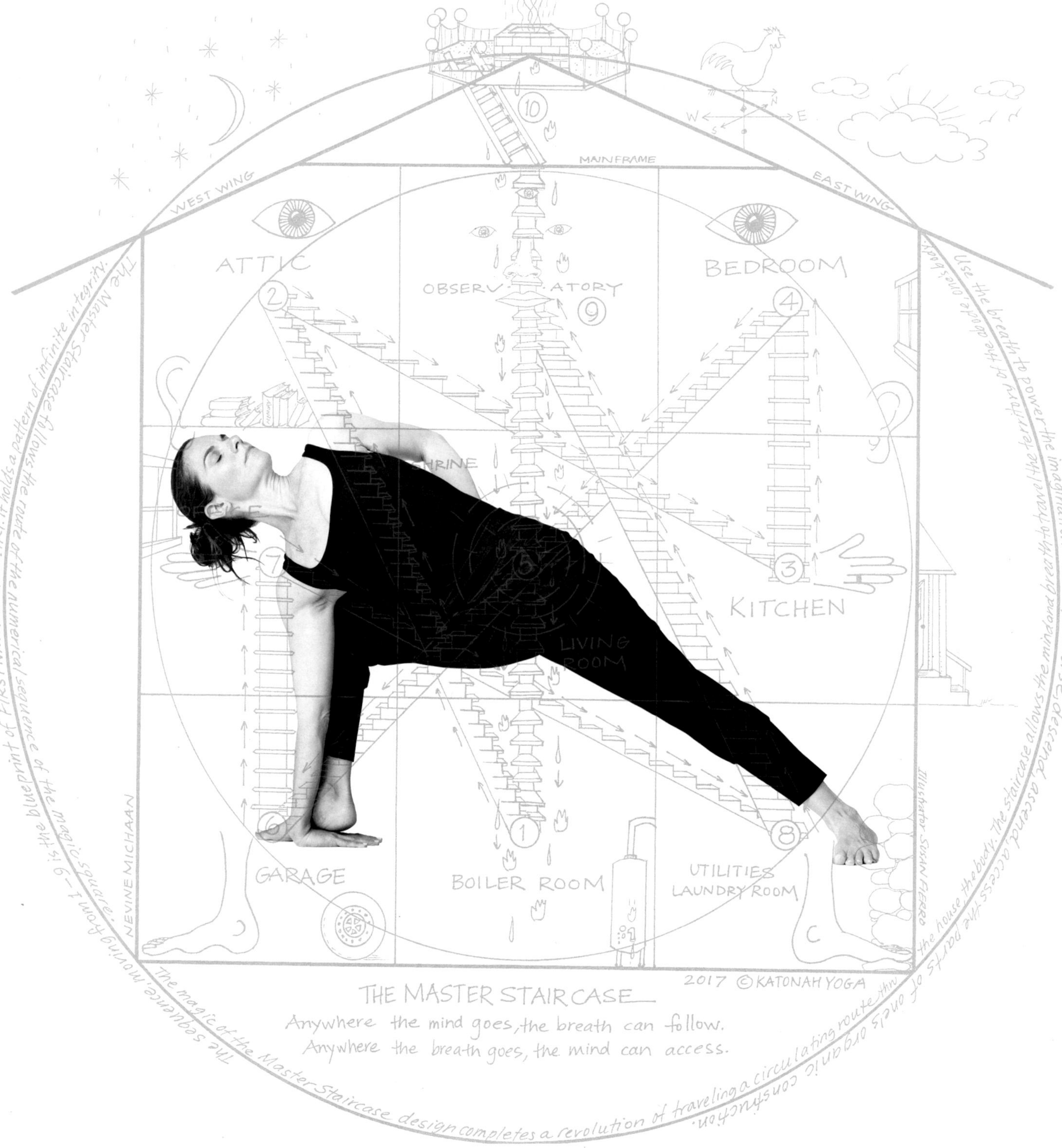

MAINFRAME
WEST WING
EAST WING
ATTIC
OBSERVATORY
BEDROOM
SHRINE
KITCHEN
LIVING ROOM
GARAGE
BOILER ROOM
UTILITIES LAUNDRY ROOM
NEVINE MICHAAN
Illustrator SUSAN FIERRO
2017 ©KATONAH YOGA
THE MASTER STAIRCASE
Anywhere the mind goes, the breath can follow.
Anywhere the breath goes, the mind can access.

THE BODY AS THE HOUSE
ABODE of the SPIRIT

An "organic construction"
A constructed organism
The Integrity of the Whole House is greater than the sum of its rooms.

10 is 1 IN A HIGER DIMENSION
TOP OF THE HEAD = MIND
eliminates heat

9 ROOMS · 3 FLOORS · 10 DOORS
IMAGINATION

The HOUSE 10 the "envelope" of a thing 5 parts
MANIPULATE MIND'S ABILITY TO USE METAPHOR FOR UNDERSTANDING
DOORS · WINDOWS · STAIRCASES
MAIN FRAME

N W E S

OUTSIDE OF HOME
SEASONS
NATURE

WEST WING
THE BODY IS THE HOUSE · JOY of LIVING IN · CARING FOR IT · WHAT THE HOME IS THE SPHERE OF ACTIVITY

EAST WING

THE FOUNDATION · ROOF · TOP

SKY LIGHT
Experience OF TIME

ATMOSPHERE OF HIGH ALTITUDE
VISION of
MEDIATED PERCEPTION
CHIMNEY

HIGH ALTITUDE

NORTHWESTERN LIGHT

PLACE of MEMORY

STAR GAZING

· BONES frame structure
· MUSCLES clay · mud sheetrock insulation

PLACE of INNOCENCE
EASTERN LIGHT

DAWNING
The New Light of the Day

SUNSET

② ATTIC
RECOLLECTION
REFLECTION

⑨ OBSERVATORY
DECONSTRUCTION
RECONSTRUCTION
VENTILATION
CALIBRATING TEMPERATURE
FIREPLACES · FURNACES and FLUES

④ BEDROOM
VISION of WAKING
AVAILABILITY OF TIME & VISION

SUN RISE

A MIND MEASURES

EYES
LINEAR
ANGULAR
REFLECTIVE
NOSTRILS
RIGHT LEFT FRONT
VISION

FLOOR 3

ROOMS E MOTE · ORGAN SYSTEMS
similar to rooms in a house
different memories, different functions, different utilities
ANGLES OF PERCEPTION

MOUTH LEADS INTO KITCHEN → LEADS
TO STOMACH · HEARTH · DIGESTION
HEAT · SPEECH · SINGING · CONVERSATION
TONGUE KEY TO THE PALET
WINDOW
AIR SENTS SMELL

DIFFERENT WINDOWS
GIVE DIFFERENT VIEWS · WALKING AROUND HOUSE ALLOWS FOR LOOKING IN BEING INSIDE THE HOUSE ALLOWS FOR LOOKING OUT

PERSPECTIVE

EARS
NW/NE
ACOUSTICS
STEREOPHONIC

WESTERN LIGHT

LIVER

MOUTH
FRONT DOOR
ANUS
BACK DOOR

REALM OF MAKING
CRAFTS
GUILDS
ABILITY

The WORLD

⑦ OFFICE
MAKE DEALS

⑤ SHRINE
LIVING ROOM

⑥ KITCHEN
DIRECTIONS
"SEASONAL"
TAKE YOU TO DIFFERENT TERRITORY

DUSK

RIGHT HAND
RIGHT ANGLE

WAY TO STAIRCASES

DAWN

DOORS

FLOOR 2

The GOAL of the THEORY is to SUPPORT your ABILITY TO LIVE in your BODY
JOYFULLY
GRACEFULLY
EFFECTIVELY
EFFICIENTLY
IMAGINATIVELY

BEST FOOT FORWARD
RISK TO GO OUT · FOOT THE BILL

ORGANIZE THE BODY
INTEGRITY OF THE ORGANIZATION
FEEDS THE OUTLOOK

ELECTRICITY
NERVOUS SYSTEM
adjust currency

CIRCUIT BREAKER

DRAINAGE
KIDNEYS

PLUMBING

WATER

FURNACE
OIL TANK

HOT WATER TANK

ROOM HAVE ATMOSPHERE
A CHARACTERISTIC

VENTILLATORY

LIGHTS

BASEMENT FOUNDATION

WALK A ROUND · CIRCUMAMBULATE THE STRUCTURE · 3 FLOORS · 9 ROOMS · 10 DOORS

STABILITY

FLOOR 1

⑥ GARAGE
GO OUT INTO THE WORLD
MOBILITY
VIRILITY
PUT FOOT TO THE PEDAL

① BOILER ROOM
PUBIS · bottom · eliminates water
VISION OF FOUNDATION
SMELL of EARTH

⑧ LAUNDRY ROOM
UTILITIES
GLANDS
adjust utilities
illustrated Susan Fierro

GO WITHIN
COME WITHOUT

4 = THE FRAME
8 = THE CUBE
9 = CONSCIOUSNESS ENCASED
5 = HALF OF THE WHOLE
10 = LEVEL TOOL OF POLARITY
15 = MEASURE OF CONSTRUCTION
20 = THE CONSTRUCTED FRAME
25 = STABILITY OF CROSS REFERENCE

by NEVINE MICHAAN 2017
KNOW YOUR BODY AS YOUR HOUSE ~ THE ABODE of YOUR SPIRIT · DEVELOP AN UNDERSTANDING OF THE BLUEPRINT OF THE ARCHETYPAL ABODE

2	9	4
7	5	3
6	1	8

©KATONAH YOGA® 2017

The MEDIATOR
LIVING · ORGANIZING · EXPLORING
MEDIATING WITH "OWN" HOUSE
EVENTUALLY ORGANIZING ABILITY TO LIVE
IN INTERNAL AND EXTERNAL SPACE
ORGANIZED BY INTELLIGENCE IN PRESCENCE
THE BODY AS THE HOUSE TO BE LIVED IN
KNOW PLUMBING · ELECTRICAL UNITS · ROOMS
UTILITIES · WINDOWS · A HOUSE IS NOT A HOME UNTIL LIVED IN.

REVELATION

GOAL SETTING
REACTION ②
REFLECTION
VISION of
the DUSK

EDIATE ⃝ VISION

POTENTIAL
VISION OF
the DAWN

HANDLES
the WORLD
⑦
RIGHT

④

HANDLES
the HEART
③
LEFT

MOBILITY

⑥

⑧
STABILITY
WILL POWER

VIRILITY

①

PATIENCE

EFFORT
TENACITY

KING OF THE MOUNTAIN

Class excerpt, Nevine Michaan, 2018

We're going to do King of the Mountain. Let me warn you: It is so easy. This is where you get to see a lot of people's techniques, too. Remember that when anybody does anything, they're pulling it out of themselves. So I'll pull out what I do, but eventually you go home and you do anything you want. First, learn it the way I teach you because it's my recipe. It's my formula. It's how I make my cookie. When I'm teaching you how to make it, that is how I want you to do it the first two or three times because I calibrated it that way. But at the end of the day, everybody goes home; everybody will do it however they want because everybody has different ingredients. People have their own recipes and directions they can add to it.

Remember, when you want to build spirit, it's communal. Spirit grows when community grows the spirit. And that's why there are lots of different spirits.

The beauty of a great King of the Mountain is the outside is very still. It is very stable. On the inside it is very dynamic. I'm going to teach you how to do all your circuits so that you don't lose your mind standing there wondering, "What am I going to do here for eight minutes?!" Well, I'm going to teach you what you're going to do there. You're going first to do grace and effort. Then we'll just switch over to the seasons; travel dawn to dusk and dusk to dawn; seize your day and your night... By the time it's done, you're going to be so well wrapped up that you're going to forget your arms are up in the air. And once you realize that you can do that, it adds all these other little things that you don't know. With your arms up in the air, all the heat will come out of your body. The heat is in the mountain and if you really open up the mountain, you see that there's a volcano in there. Also, the water goes down the mountain. So if you have too much water in you, it's going to start pouring out.

Tadasana is a mountain. Bring your feet together. Place your tongue lightly in the center of your upper palette. Bring your knees together. Bring your ankles together. Keep moving. Occupy center, mediate circumference. The goal is to be the sovereign of your dominion. Follow your breathing. Close your eyes. Inhale and exhale. Both knees ski to 2 o'clock. Your heart knows it wants to sing to an audience. The liver at 2 o'clock travels around memory and feeds the heart at ten o'clock. Your kidneys are now level and your lungs are at a perfect spot. So now you can open up your windows, get enough air and be in the middle of yourself.

Interlace your fingers. Palms up, bring your blocks overhead. This is your crown. The big trick is don't drop the block. Open your imagination. Send the line from the universe all the way through you: your throat, your torso, your perineum. Descend it into the earth so that you occupy the center of your sphere. Potential in front. Memories behind. Grace is descending. Effort is ascending. And everything is happening around you. So if you know grace and effort, grace descends in front of you as water, effort ascends up your back as fire. So be graceful and make your efforts. Smile. Only because an inner smile is incredibly radiant and it radiates your chemistry in the subtlest way. That's why the minute somebody's smiling at you, you react. So remember you're not smiling at anybody. They might think you are but you're not. You're just smiling because it gives it to you. You do it for you. Take your time.

When you're in the heels of your feet, you are in your past. In the balls of your feet, you are in your future. Present becomes memory. Memories push your forwards and you become reflective. Keep moving. Front is your future, behind you are your memories and, in the middle, is your present.

Be present. Keep moving. Inhale, let spring rise. Hold your breath. Let summer ripen. Exhale, let autumn descend, be empty for winter, and then do it again. Most of it is, deal. Deal, deal, deal, deal, deal. Know what to remember. Know what to forget. Forget how hard it is. Remember you're going to get through it. At the end, you will totally forget it was hard because you will have gotten through it. Know that time spins from dawn on your left out in front of you to your dusk on your right, and from dusk behind your to back to your dawn.

Keep everything in mind. If you don't know how to read a clock, you might be there at the right place but at the wrong time. If you only know how to read a clock, you might arrive at the right time but at the wrong place.

Organize yourself. When you're well-organized, you get ease. It is easier on the heart; your vision is clear; you have options. So what is this for? It is to really own nature. To know how the elements work. How to hold it together. And how to really achieve dominion as you practice. Isn't that a nice trick?

REVELATION

10

GRACE

9

MEDIATED VISION

REACTION
REFLECTION
GOAL SETTING

POTENTIAL

VISION of
the DUSK

VISION of
the DAWN

HANDLES
the WORLD

7

HANDLES the
HEART

3

RIGHT

LEFT

5

STABILITY
WILL POWER

8

MOBILITY

6

VIRILITY

PATIENCE

EFFORT
TENACITY

I do one practice that I really love to teach.
I do tadasana. I bring my feet together,
ankles together, and knees together. And I put
my hands webbed like this (fingers interlaced),
and I put them up there, holding up a block.
I put on music for eleven minutes (or 9, or 5).
And I make sure that I don't drop the block.

I have to learn how to hover, how to be there.
How to magic square my hands,
how to magic square my feet, how to orient.
I do everything I can! But I don't get to leave
the pose. That's a very good way to learn
a private practice. Pick a piece of music
you like and don't stop until it's done.

To own the mountain is to own the sovereignty of your dominion.
It is not male. It is not female. It is really about being generative in Great Nature.
What you are doing when you meditating is manipulating
your chemistry. It's like when you go into a mountain and you start
seeing that there is a a volcano in there.

1—9
Grace reigns.
It descends from above as water.
Effort is ascending as fire from below,
the first polarity is
between grace and effort.
As you inhale, let your efforts
rise up in your memories.
As you exhale,
let the grace descend.
in your potential.

2—8
Inhale, let spring rise.
Hold your breath, let summer
ripen overhead. Exhale,
let autumn descend as
memories behind you.
Be empty, find the
insights of winter.
And then inhale again.

When a volcano erupts, it's shocking how alive and how much
Great Nature is in that mountain. On the surface you are just seeing trees
and flowers and stuff. Inside it is seething.
When you erupt that mountain, you are releasing
a tremendous amount of energy.

3–7
Know time.
Time is always traveling
from the heart side towards the liver,
from the liver around the
back, back to the heart.
Be revolutionary.
Use time to your advantage.
Use fire to your advantage.
Use water to your advantage.
And put yourself in the middle
of all of it.

4–6
Day and Night; waking
and sleeping.
Souls descend, spirits
ascend in sleep.
In the morning light you
get up and see.
At night, your spirit
rises as your body rests in sleep.

5
The polarity of 5 is 5,
and what that means is
the polarity of oneself is reflection.
Self-reflect. The only way to find the two ends
of self is self-reflecting oneself. But the big joke
of 5 reflecting itself is it flips
from being polarity to trinity.
The minute you reflect on yourself,
the dialogue moves from being 2 to 3
because there is always space between.
The minute you put 5 in the middle,
we change the whole narrative
from polarity
to trinity.

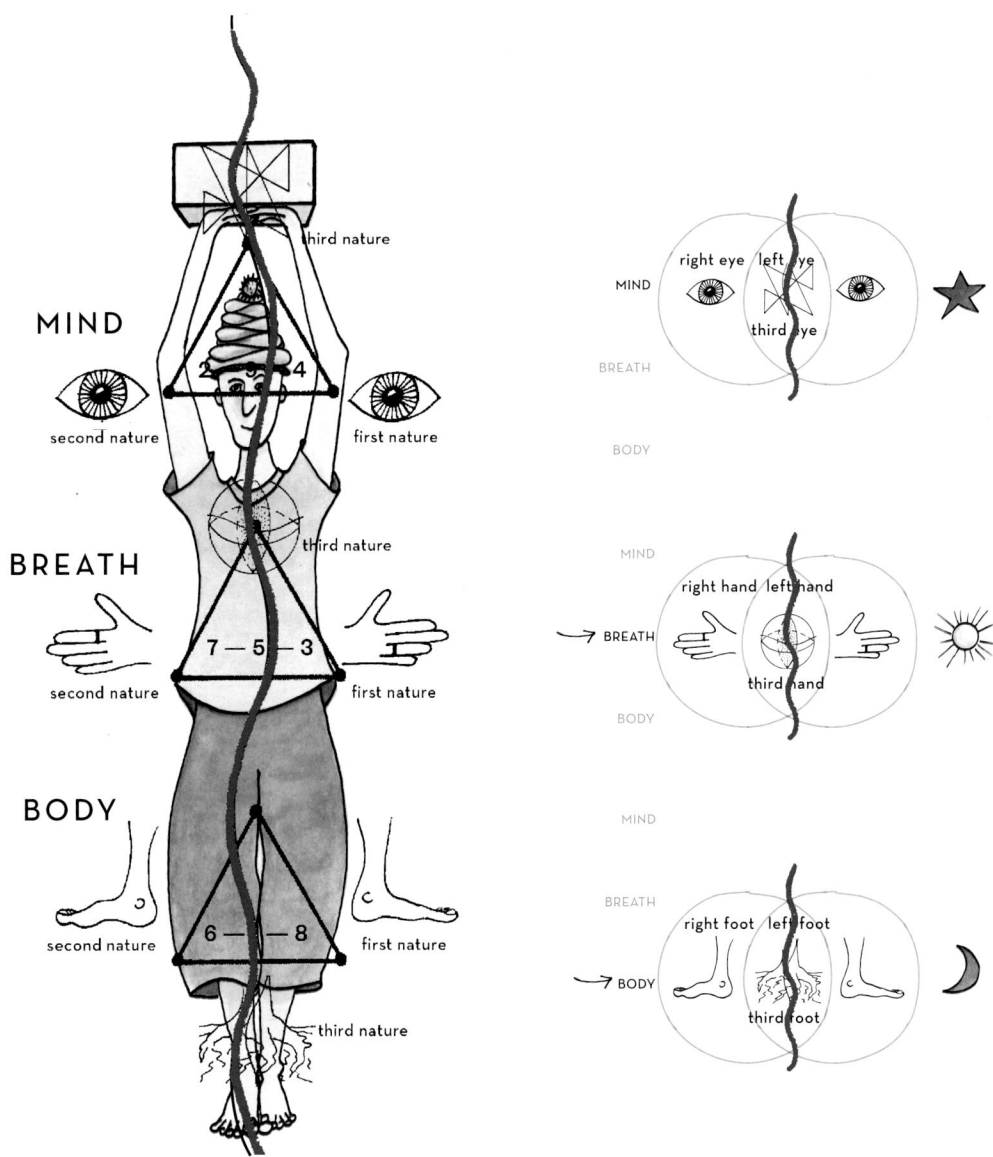

MIND

second nature · first nature

BREATH

second nature · first nature

BODY

second nature · first nature

third nature

MIND · BREATH · BODY

right eye / left eye · third eye

right hand / left hand · third hand

right foot / left foot · third foot

MOVING FROM THE EXPLICIT TO THE IMPLICIT

In the body, what is Explicit is obvious: two eyes, two hands, two feet. It's what is seen, heard, touched, produced. The Explicit represents First and Second Natures.

By contrast, what is Implicit in the body is what is not seen. It's the 3rd eye, 3rd hand, 3rd foot. It is the thinking process: choosing, adjusting, mediating, manipulating, and meditating. It is the imaginative current connecting the personal to the universal, the Golden Thread. The Implicit represents Third Nature.

The First Nature is lunar, organic. The Second Nature is solar, acquired. The Third Nature is stellar. In every piece of you all three natures are represented—the current and currency of self-expression.

What is explicit has polarity in it. What is implicit is the mediation of the polarities.

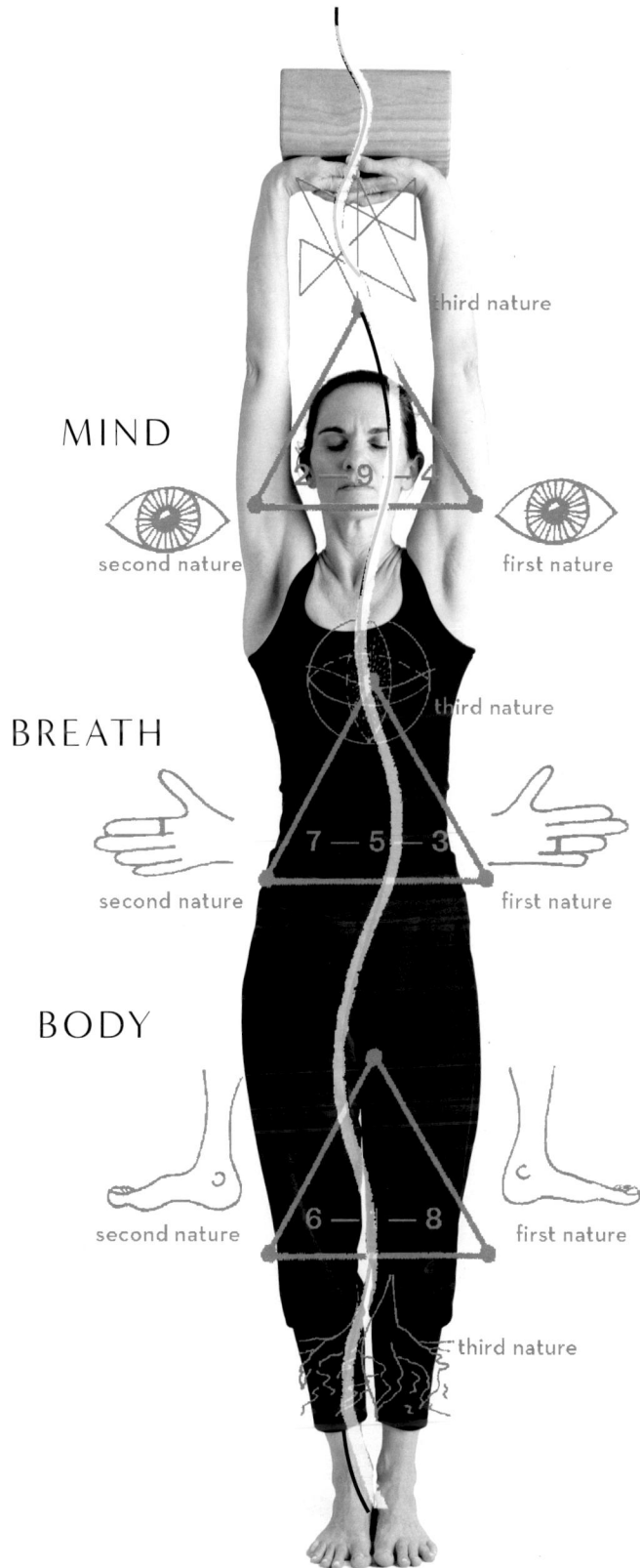

MIND

third nature

second nature   first nature

BREATH

third nature

second nature   first nature

BODY

second nature   first nature

third nature

ANY WHOLE CAN BE DIVIDED INTO ITS NINE COMPOSITE PARTS

Bottom, middle top, left, right, center, potential, past, present. That is the magic square. Or, rather, the magic cube. You are the magic cube. In front of you is your future. Behind you are your memories. In the middle of you is your presence.

The middle of you articulates. And the top of you is trying to figure out the big picture. Left side, you have an inheritance. Right side, you have an education. And in the middle, you have a soul. In front of you and behind you, know that you're playing time.

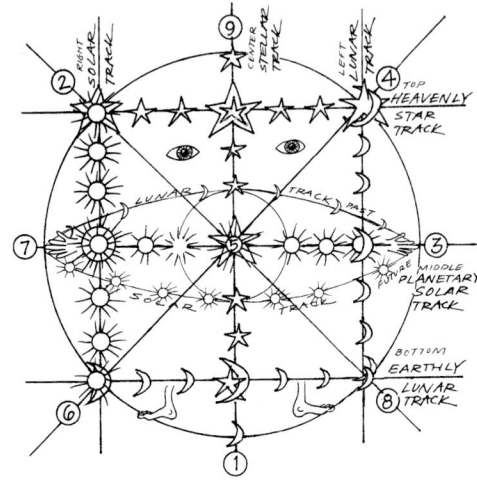

EMBODIMENT OF SOLAR LUNAR STELLAR

Yoga is about being powerful. Your power is using your body, your mind, your breath. It is your scholasticism. It's your lunacy. It's your stellar nature. You have all of it in you.

THE EPITOME OF ☆☆☽ OF THE 9 CONSTITUENT PARTS OF A BODY

7	8	9
SOLAR OF SOLAR	LUNAR OF LUNAR	STELLAR OF STELLAR
SOLAR ON RIGHT	LUNAR ON LEFT	STELLAR IN CENTER
SOLAR IN MIDDLE	LUNAR ON BOTTOM	STELLAR ON TOP
SOLAR IN FUTURE	LUNAR IN PAST	STELLAR IN PRESENT
TECHNIQUE: LEARN TO MAKE THE DEAL	INHERITANCE: OWNING THE EMBODIMENT	FULFILLMENT: ACHIEVING THE VISION

CURRENCY OF PERSONAL NATURE

Breath and meditation practices can be organized following the circuitry of the integrated fit, the figure 8. All fronts have backs, all backs have fronts— making the present available.

When you fold bodies, you don't fold bodies in half because bodies are designed not with only the front and back. A body is designed with a front and a back and an inside, so the body folds in thirds. Paper folds in half. When you fold paper, you play it for folding origami. But when you play with bodies, you play for fitting. Origami is asana for paper and asana is origami for bodies.

How do you fit in the present? In between your past and your future would be fitting in the present. That's a good thing to learn. So the big piece on that one is this. When you really want to be present, you step back. You don't step forwards because when you step forwards what you're really doing is bracing yourself for your future. But when you step back, you can see the present of your past and the present of your future, and you will be in the middle.

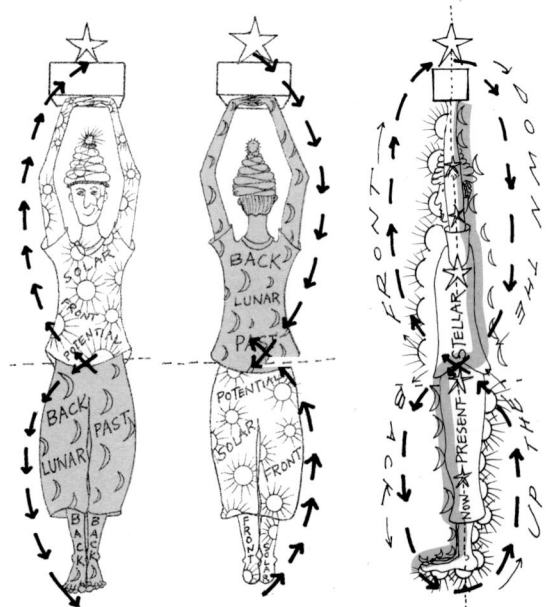

SPACE

Six divisions represent Space: bottom, middle, and top, right, left, and center.

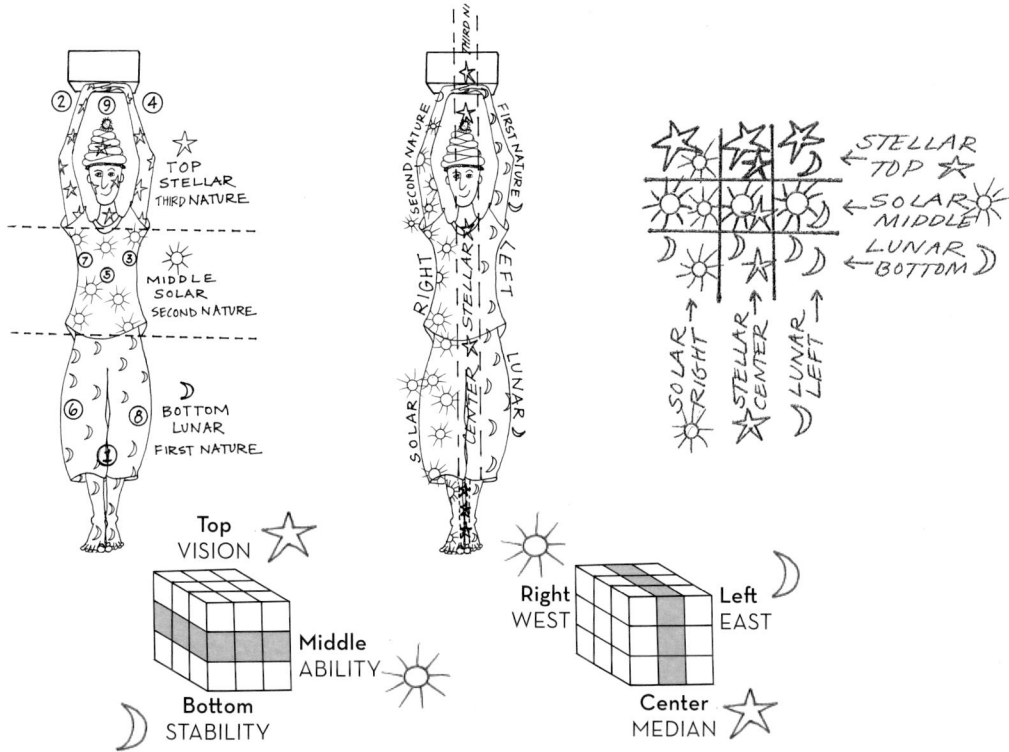

TOP
STELLAR
THIRD NATURE

MIDDLE
SOLAR
SECOND NATURE

BOTTOM
LUNAR
FIRST NATURE

THIRD NATURE
SECOND NATURE
FIRST NATURE
RIGHT
CENTER STELLAR
LEFT LUNAR
SOLAR

STELLAR TOP ★
SOLAR MIDDLE
LUNAR BOTTOM

SOLAR RIGHT
STELLAR CENTER
LUNAR LEFT

Top
VISION ★

Middle
ABILITY

Bottom
STABILITY

Right
WEST

Left
EAST

Center
MEDIAN ★

TIME

What is in the front? The future. What is in the back? The past. What is in the middle? The moment. So stay a moment. Manipulate the potential and the memory. Rise above yourself. Descend below yourself. Mediate yourself.

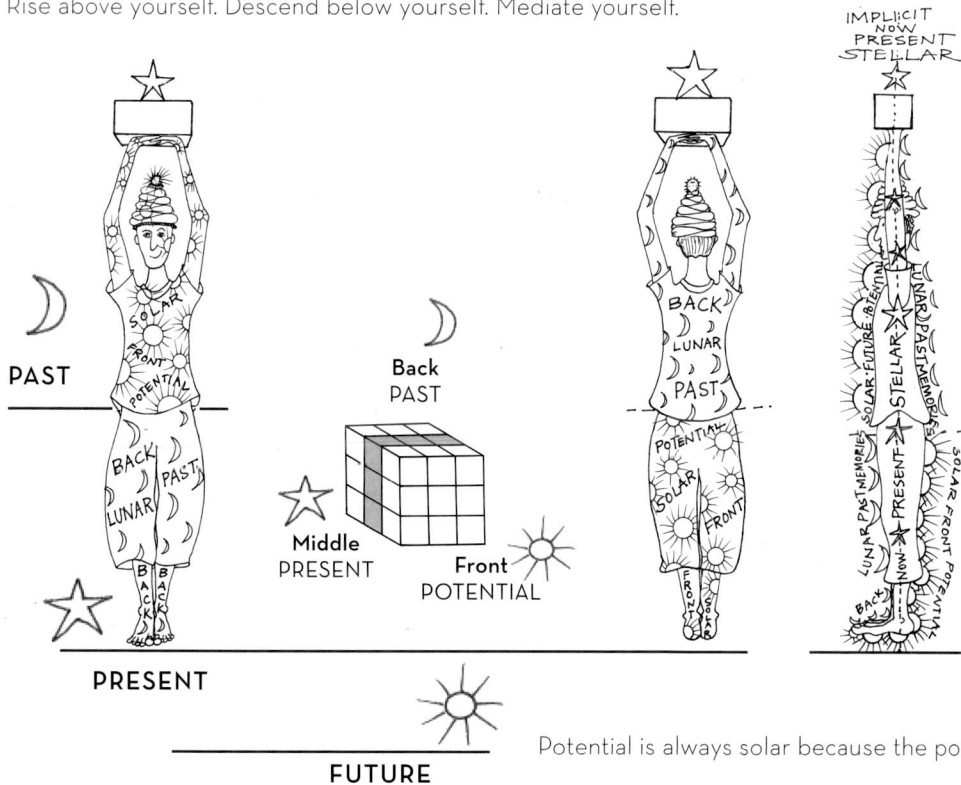

PAST

PRESENT

FUTURE

SOLAR
FRONT
POTENTIAL
BACK
LUNAR
PAST
BACK

Middle
PRESENT

Front
POTENTIAL

Back
PAST

BACK
LUNAR
PAST
POTENTIAL
SOLAR
FRONT

IMPLICIT
NOW
PRESENT
STELLAR

SOLAR FUTURE
LUNAR PAST MEMORIES
STELLAR
NOW PRESENT
LUNAR PAST MEMORIES
SOLAR FRONT POTENTIAL
BACK

Potential is always solar because the potential follows the light.

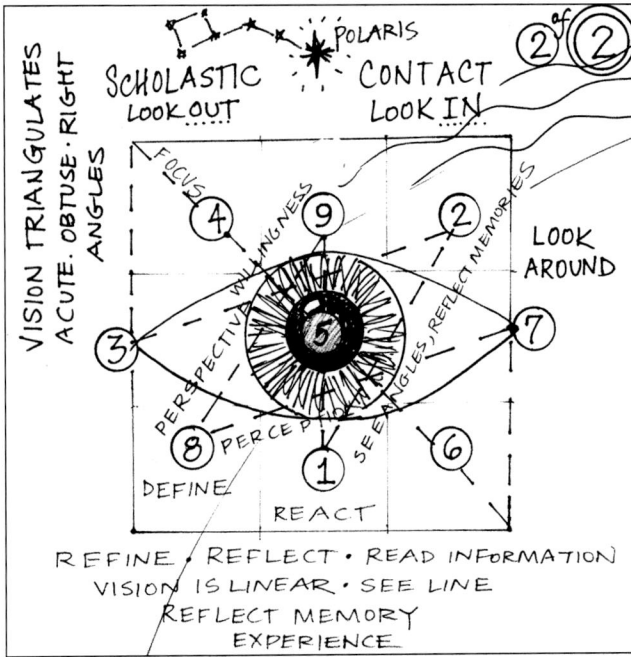

RIGHT EYE

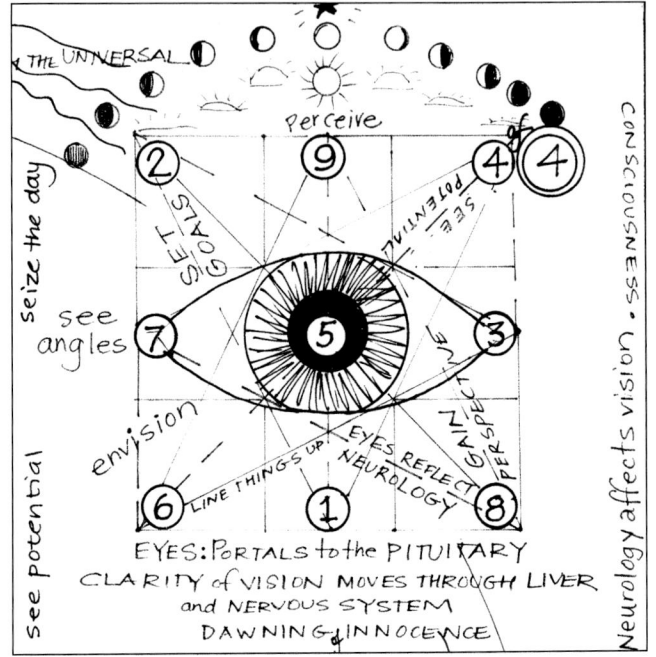

LEFT EYE

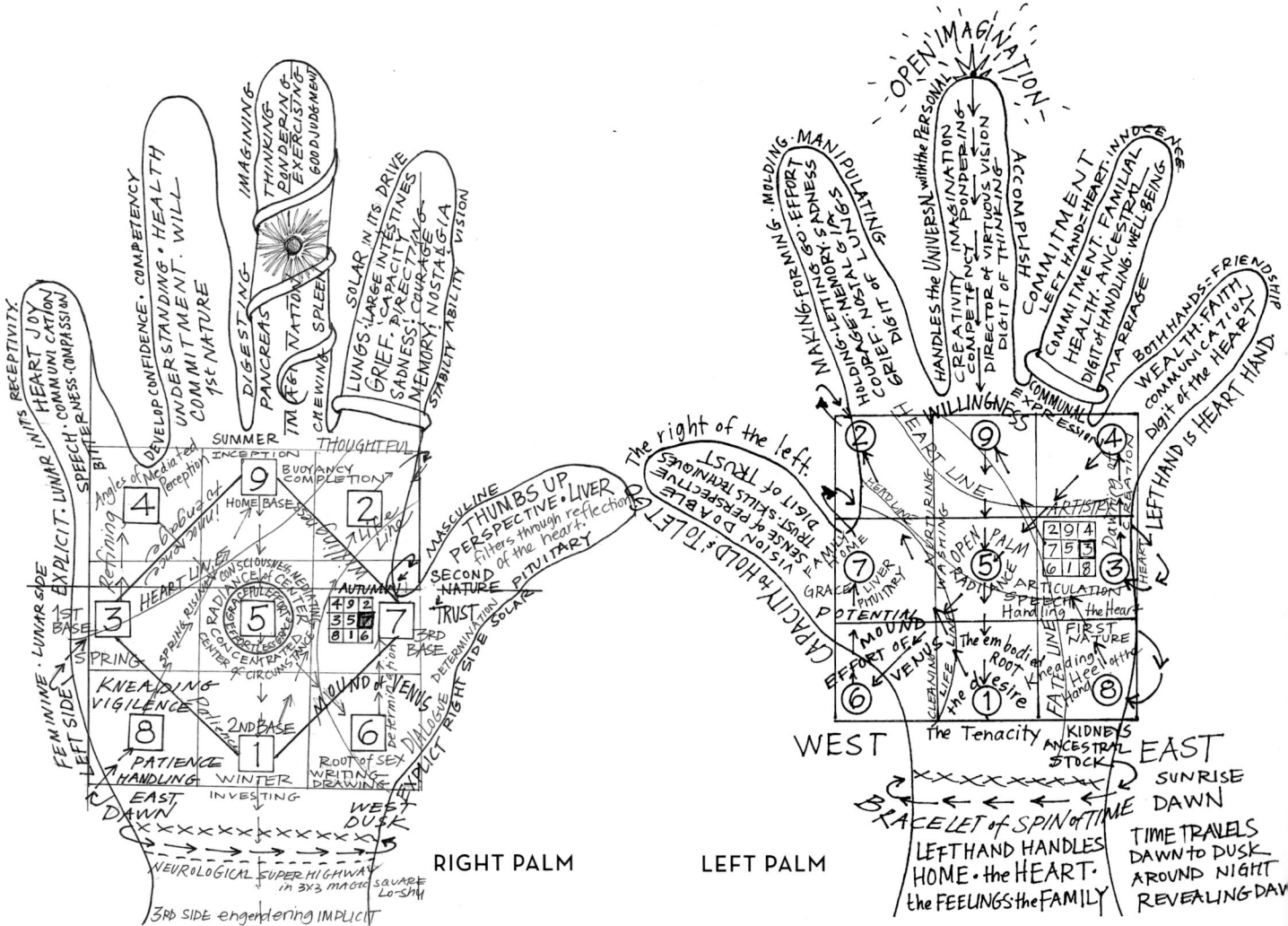

RIGHT PALM

LEFT PALM

Know only your right foot! 1, find the heel of the right. 2, go forwards, forwards, forwards, find the ball and big toe of the right foot. 3, find the outer arch of the right foot. 4, go forwards, forwards, forwards, find the little toe of the right foot. 5, find the middle of the right foot. 6, find the inner heel of the right foot. 7, find the inner arch of the right foot. 8, find the outer heel of the right foot. 9, find the middle toe of the right foot. 10, own your foot.

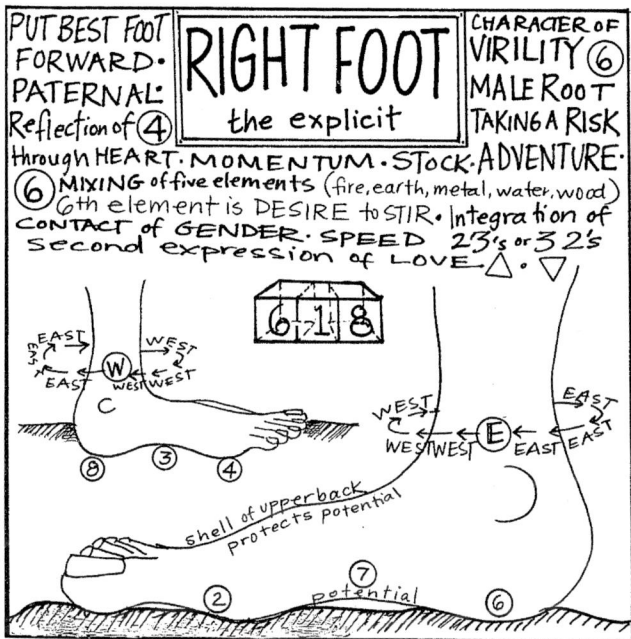

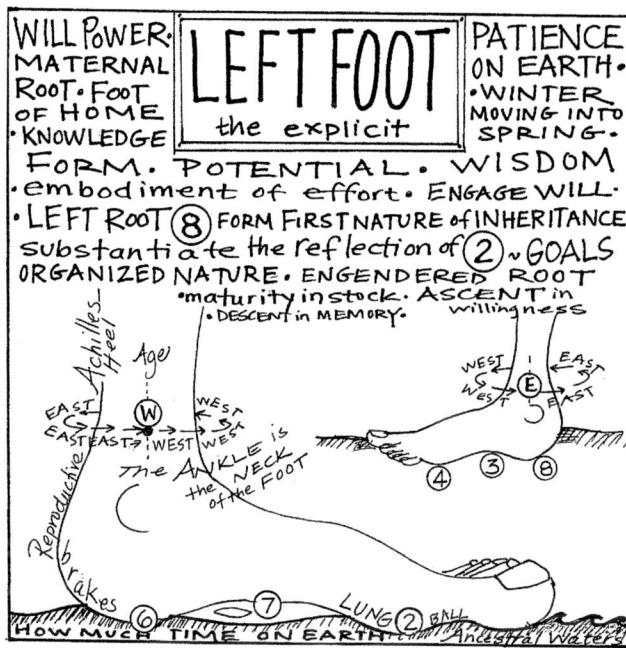

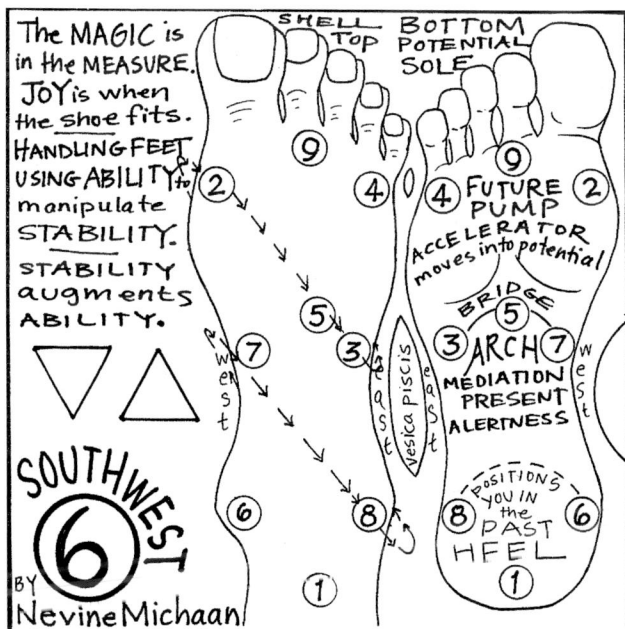

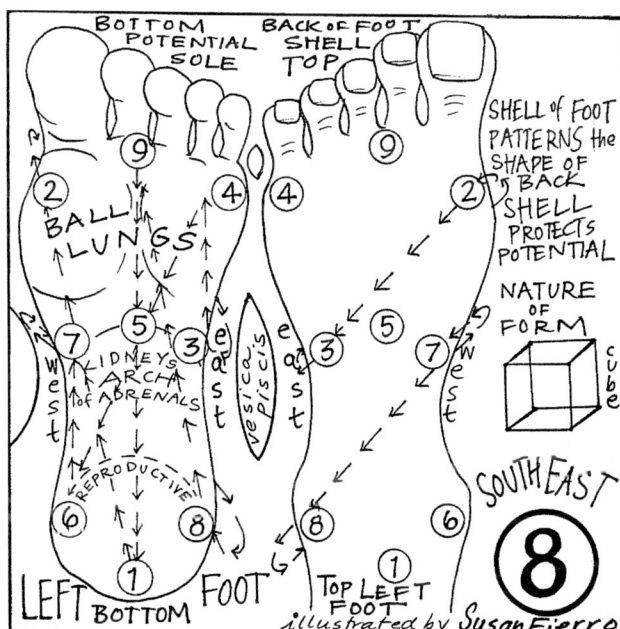

RIGHT FOOT
the explicit

PUT BEST FOOT FORWARD. PATERNAL. Reflection of ④ through HEART. MOMENTUM. STOCK. ADVENTURE.

CHARACTER OF VIRILITY ⑥ MALE ROOT TAKING A RISK

⑥ MIXING of five elements (fire, earth, metal, water, wood) 6th element is DESIRE to STIR. Integration of CONTACT of GENDER. SPEED 2 3's or 3 2's second expression of LOVE △ ▽

6 · 1 · 8

EAST WEST EAST WEST WEST
W
C
⑧ ③ ④
WEST WEST WEST E EAST EAST EAST
shell of upperback Protects potential
② potential ⑥

LEFT FOOT
the explicit

WILL POWER. MATERNAL ROOT. FOOT OF HOME · KNOWLEDGE

PATIENCE ON EARTH. · WINTER MOVING INTO SPRING.

FORM. POTENTIAL. WISDOM · embodiment of effort. ENGAGE WILL. · LEFT ROOT ⑧ FORM FIRST NATURE of INHERITANCE substantiate the reflection of ② ~ GOALS ORGANIZED NATURE. ENGENDERED ROOT · maturity in stock. ASCENT in · DESCENT in MEMORY. willingness

Achilles Heel Age
EAST EAST WEST WEST WEST
W
The ANKLE is the NECK of the FOOT
Reproductive brakes
⑥ ⑦ LUNG ② BALL
HOW MUCH TIME ON EARTH Ancestral Waters
WEST WEST EAST EAST E
④ ③

The MAGIC is in the MEASURE. JOY is when the shoe fits. HANDLING FEET USING ABILITY to manipulate STABILITY.

STABILITY augments ABILITY.

SHELL TOP BOTTOM POTENTIAL SOLE
⑨ ⑨
② ④ ④ FUTURE PUMP ② ACCELERATOR moves into potential
BRIDGE
⑤ ⑤
⑦ ⑦ ③ ③ ARCH ⑦
west vesica piscis MEDIATION PRESENT ALERTNESS
⑥ ⑧ ⑧ POSITIONS YOU in the PAST HEEL ⑥
① ①

SOUTHWEST ⑥ BY Nevine Michaan

BOTTOM POTENTIAL SOLE BACK OF FOOT SHELL TOP
② ⑨ ④ ④ ⑨ ②
BALL LUNGS
2nd west ⑦ ⑤ ③ e/a/s/t vesica piscis e/a/s/t ③ ⑤ ⑦ West
KIDNEYS ARCH of ADRENALS
REPRODUCTIVE
⑥ ⑧ ⑧ ⑥
① ①
LEFT BOTTOM FOOT TOP LEFT FOOT

SHELL of FOOT PATTERNS the SHAPE of BACK SHELL PROTECTS POTENTIAL

NATURE OF FORM

cube

SOUTHEAST ⑧

illustrated by Susan Fierro

Find your left foot. 1, find the heel of the left foot. Because you don't travel everywhere. Go to one place. 2, find the ball and big toe of the left foot. 3, find the outer arch of the left foot. 4, find the pinky of the left foot. 5, find the middle. 6, inner heel, inner heel, Mount of Venus. 7, find the inner arch. 8, outer heel. 9, second toe. Put it all together.

KATONAH YOGA MAPS

Full set of maps can be found in the Maps, Charts and Meditations Manual.

TRAVELING THE SUPERHIGHWAY

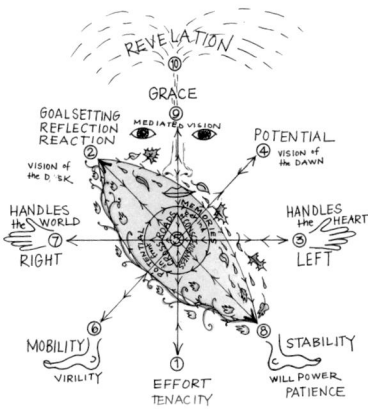

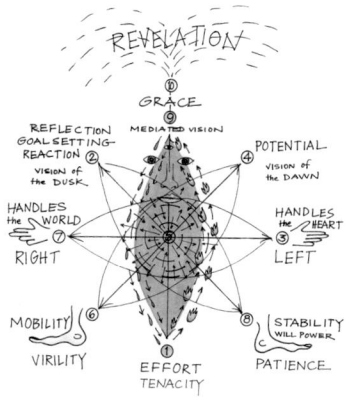

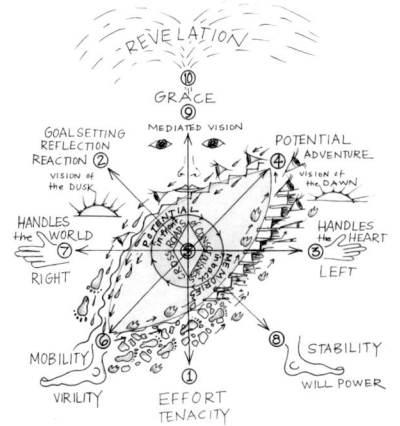

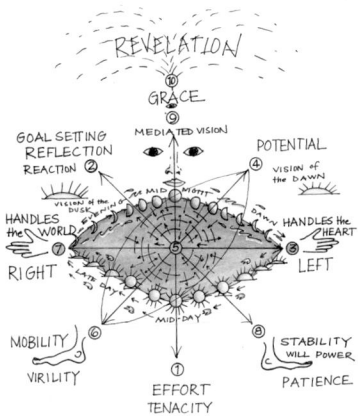

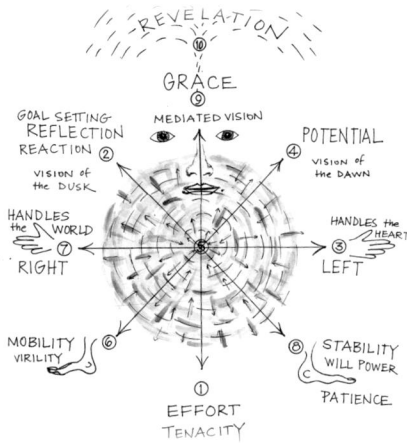

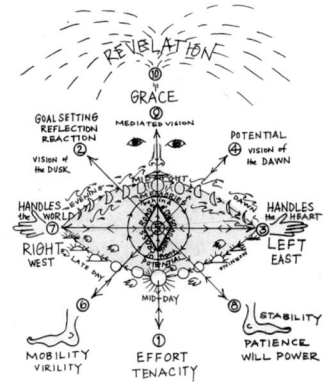

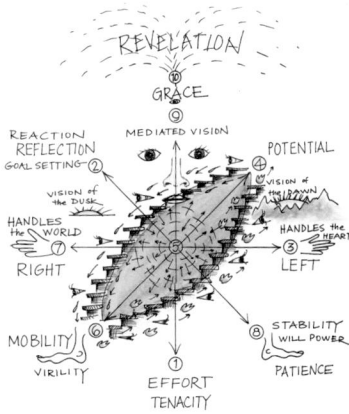

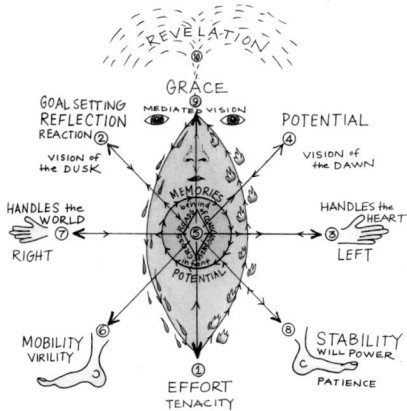

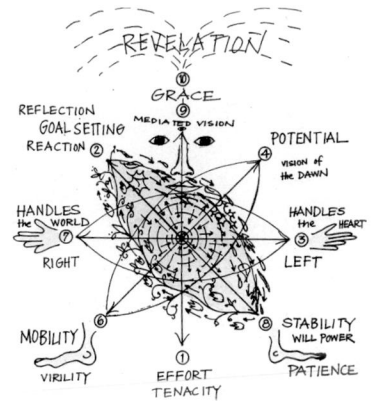

COMPASS ROSES

COMPASS OF THE SEASONS

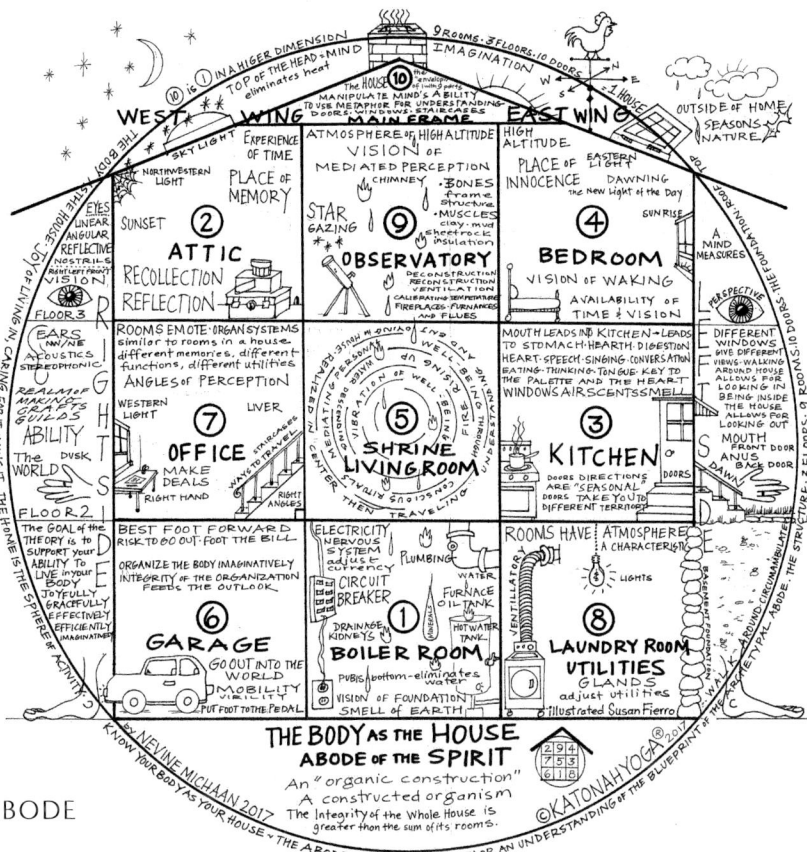

BLUEPRINT OF THE ABODE

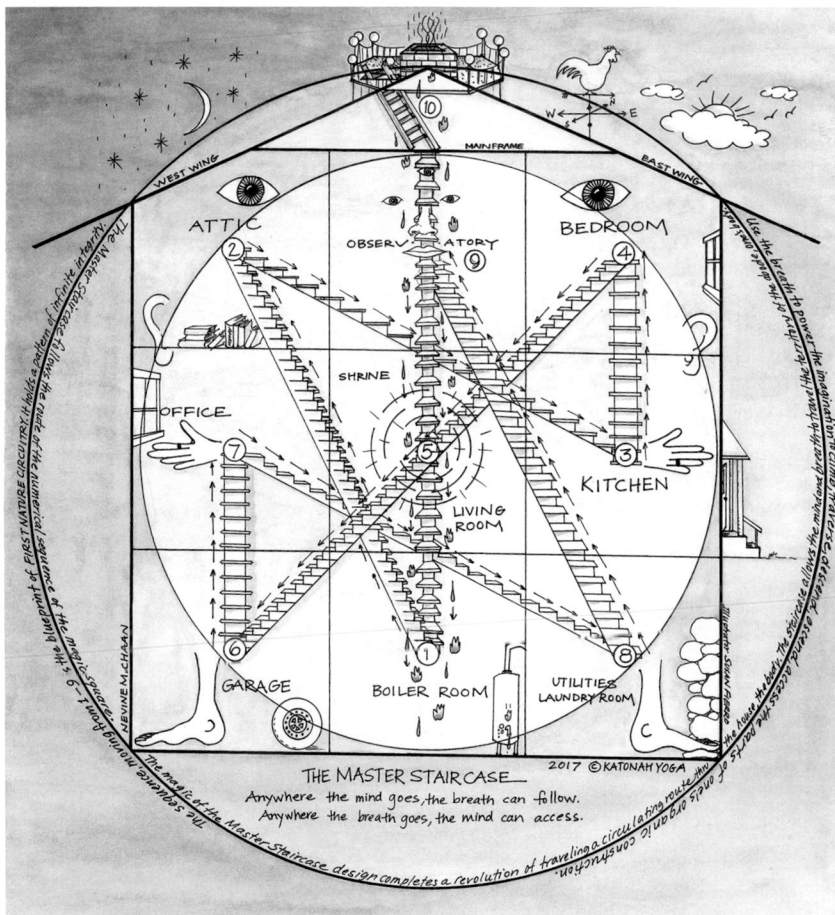

THE MASTER STAIRCASE

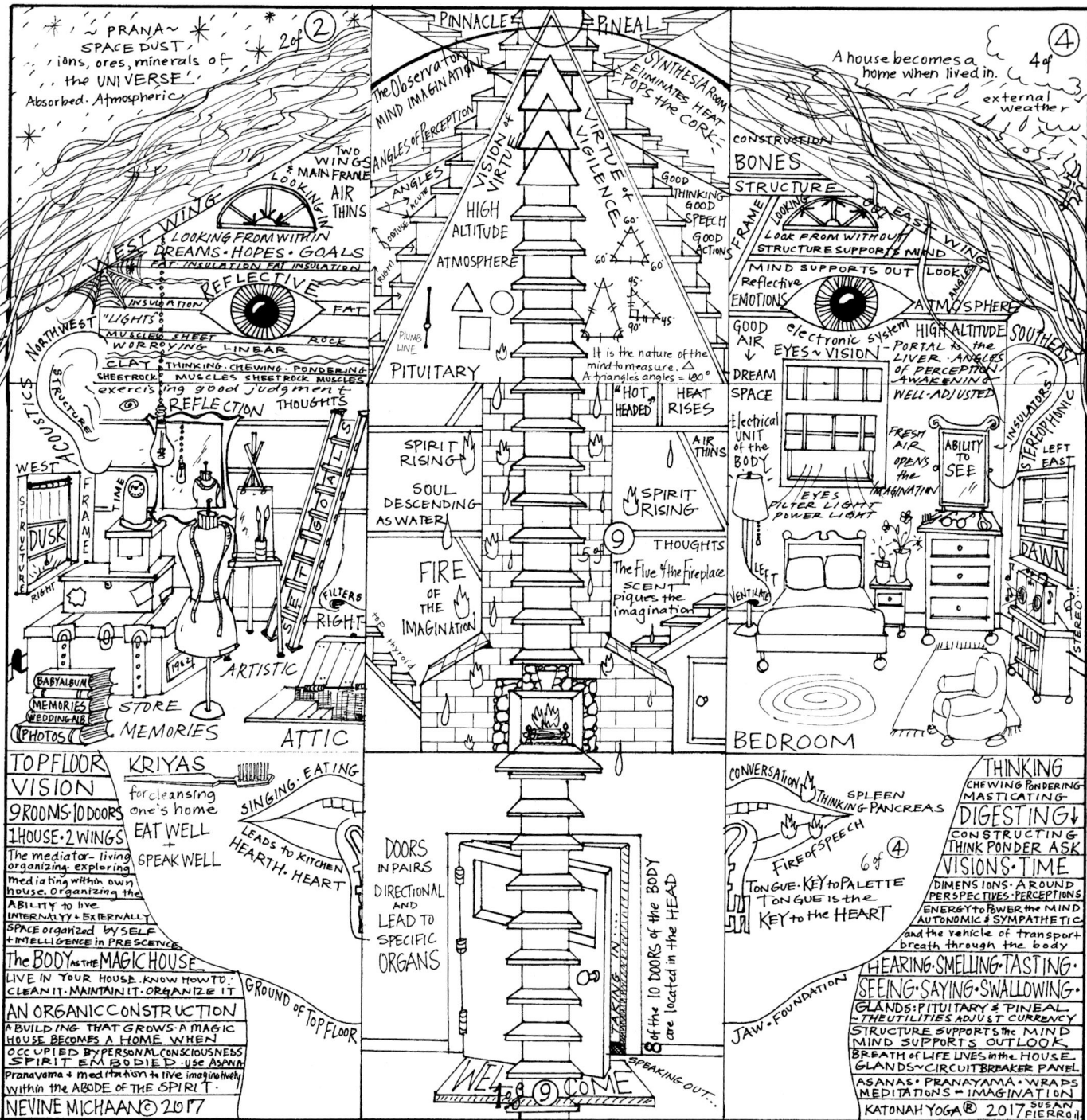

~PRANA~
SPACE DUST
ions, ores, minerals of
the UNIVERSE
Absorbed · Atmospheric

A house becomes a home when lived in.
external weather

PINNACLE · PINEAL

The Observatory
MIND · IMAGINATION
ANGLES OF PERCEPTION

SYNTHESIA ROOM
ELIMINATES HEAT
~POPS the CORK~

CONSTRUCTION
BONES
STRUCTURE
FRAME · LOOKING OUT · EAST WING

TWO WINGS & MAIN FRAME
LOOKING IN
AIR THINS

VISION & VIRTUE

VIRTUE & VIGILANCE

Good THINKING
GOOD SPEECH
GOOD ACTIONS

LOOK FROM WITHOUT
STRUCTURE SUPPORTS MIND
MIND SUPPORTS OUT · LOOK

WEST WING
LOOKING FROM WITHIN
DREAMS · HOPES · GOALS

HIGH ALTITUDE
ATMOSPHERE

Reflective
EMOTIONS

HIGH ALTITUDE
PORTAL to the
LIVER · ANGLES
of PERCEPTION
AWAKENING
WELL-ADJUSTED

FAT INSULATION FAT INSULATION
REFLECTIVE
INSULATION FAT
NORTHWEST "LIGHTS"
MUSCLED SHEET
WORROYING LINEAR
CLAY
SHEETROCK
THINKING · CHEWING · PONDERING
MUSCLES SHEETROCK MUSCLES
exercising good judgment
REFLECTION THOUGHTS

It is the nature of the mind to measure. △
A triangle's angles = 180°

GOOD AIR

electronic system
EYES ~ VISION

DREAM SPACE

ABILITY TO SEE

SOUTHEAST

STEREOPHONIC

ACOUSTICS
STRUCTURE

WEST FRAME
DUSK
RIGHT
1964

TIME

LINEAR

"HOT HEADED" · HEAT RISES

AIR THINS

SPIRIT RISING
SOUL DESCENDING AS WATER

SPIRIT RISING

THOUGHTS

Electrical UNIT of the BODY

EYES FILTER LIGHT
POWER LIGHT

LEFT

FRESH AIR OPENS the IMAGINATION

LEFT EAST

DAWN

VENTILATE

FILTERS RIGHT

FIRE OF THE IMAGINATION

The Flue of the fireplace SCENT piques the imagination

ARTISTIC

BABY ALBUM
MEMORIES
WEDDING N.B.
PHOTOS
STORE MEMORIES

ATTIC

BEDROOM

TOP FLOOR VISION
9 ROOMS · 10 DOORS
1 HOUSE · 2 WINGS
The mediator- living organizing· exploring mediating within own house. Organizing the ABILITY to live INTERNALLY + EXTERNALLY SPACE organized by SELF + INTELLIGENCE in PRESENCE

KRIYAS
for cleansing one's home
EAT WELL + SPEAK WELL

SINGING· EATING

LEADS to kitchen
HEARTH· HEART

DOORS IN PAIRS
DIRECTIONAL AND LEAD TO SPECIFIC ORGANS

CONVERSATION
THINKING
SPLEEN
THINKING PANCREAS
FIRE of SPEECH

THINKING
CHEWING PONDERING MASTICATING
DIGESTING
CONSTRUCTING THINK PONDER ASK
VISIONS · TIME
DIMENSIONS · AROUND PERSPECTIVES · PERCEPTIONS
ENERGY to POWER the MIND AUTONOMIC & SYMPATHETIC
and the vehicle of transport breath through the body

Tongue· KEY to PALETTE
TONGUE is the KEY to the HEART

The BODY as the MAGIC HOUSE
LIVE IN YOUR HOUSE· KNOW HOW TO: CLEAN IT· MAINTAIN IT· ORGANIZE IT

GROUND OF TOP FLOOR

6 of 4

TAKING IN...

of the 10 DOORS of the BODY are located in the HEAD

HEARING· SMELLING· TASTING·
SEEING· SAYING· SWALLOWING·
GLANDS: PITUITARY & PINEAL
- THE UTILITIES ADJUST CURRENCY
STRUCTURE SUPPORTS the MIND
MIND SUPPORTS OUTLOOK
BREATH of LIFE LIVES in the HOUSE
GLANDS ~ CIRCUIT BREAKER PANEL
ASANAS· PRANAYAMA · WRAPS
MEDITATIONS = IMAGINATION

AN ORGANIC CONSTRUCTION
A BUILDING THAT GROWS· A MAGIC HOUSE BECOMES A HOME WHEN OCCUPIED BY PERSONAL CONSCIOUSNESS SPIRIT EMBODIED · use ASANA
Pranayama + meditation to live imaginatively within the ABODE of the SPIRIT

SPEAKING OUT...

WEL 9 COME

JAW· FOUNDATION

NEVINE MICHAAN © 2017

KATONAH YOGA ® 2017 SUSAN FIERRO

TOP FLOOR

BACK OF HEAD

PALIMPSESTIC MAPS

Our maps are symbols of enneagons— they can be drawn within a 3 x 3 grid as well as
on an eight-spoke wheel. When overlaid on each other our maps reveal deeper patterns.

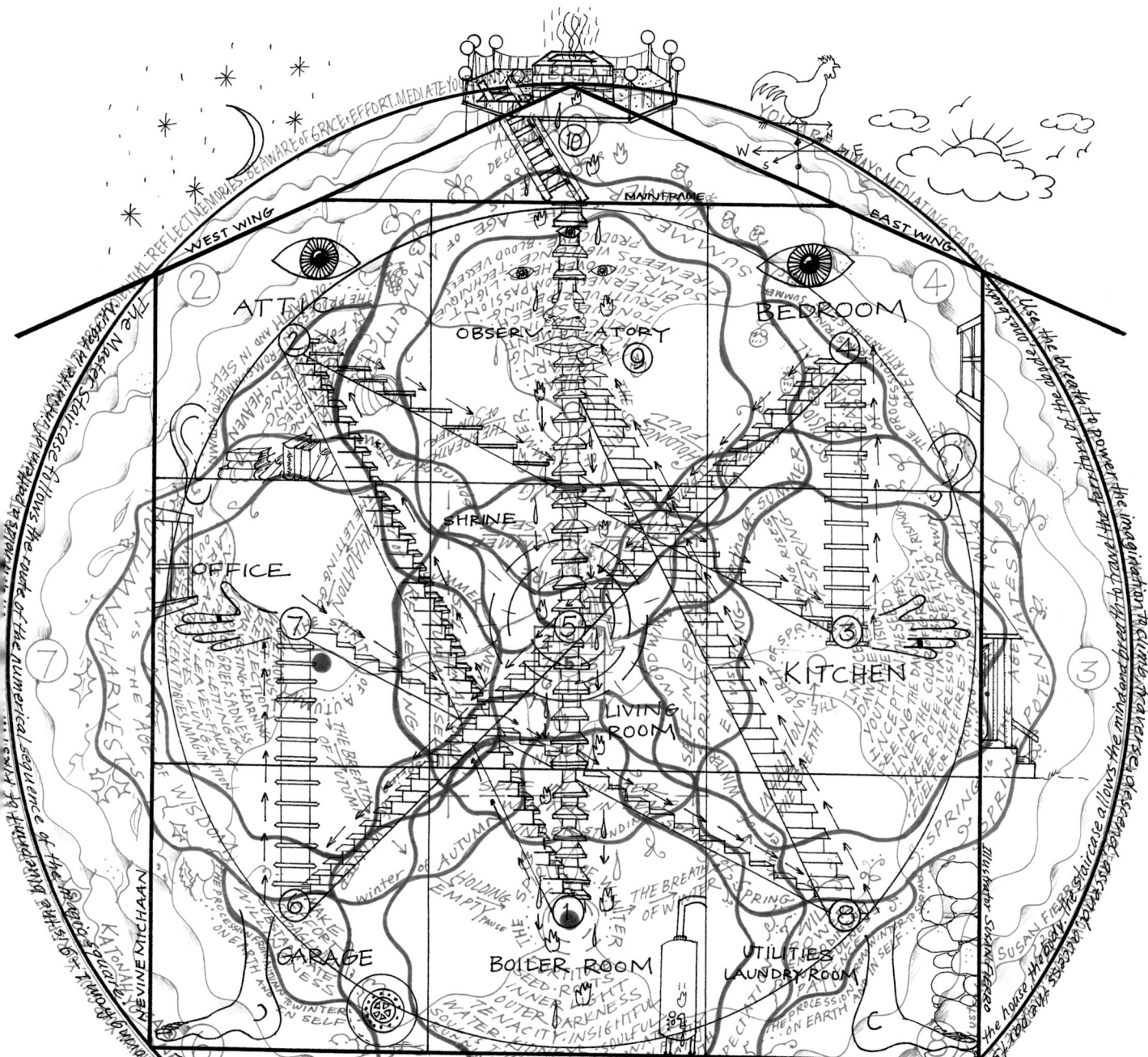

THE MASTER STAIRCASE

Anywhere the mind goes, the breath can follow.
Anywhere the breath goes, the mind can access.

2017 © KATONAH YOGA

WEST WING   MAIN FRAME   EAST WING

ATTIC

OBSERVATORY

BEDROOM

SHRINE

OFFICE

KITCHEN

LIVING
ROOM

GARAGE

BOILER ROOM

UTILITIES
LAUNDRY ROOM

N W S E

1 2 3 4 5 6 7 8 9 10

FIRE ALWAYS RISES

THE BREATH OF WINTER

FEED ROOM
INNER LIGHT
OUTER DARKNESS
TENACITY, INSIGHTFUL
WATER, SOULFUL

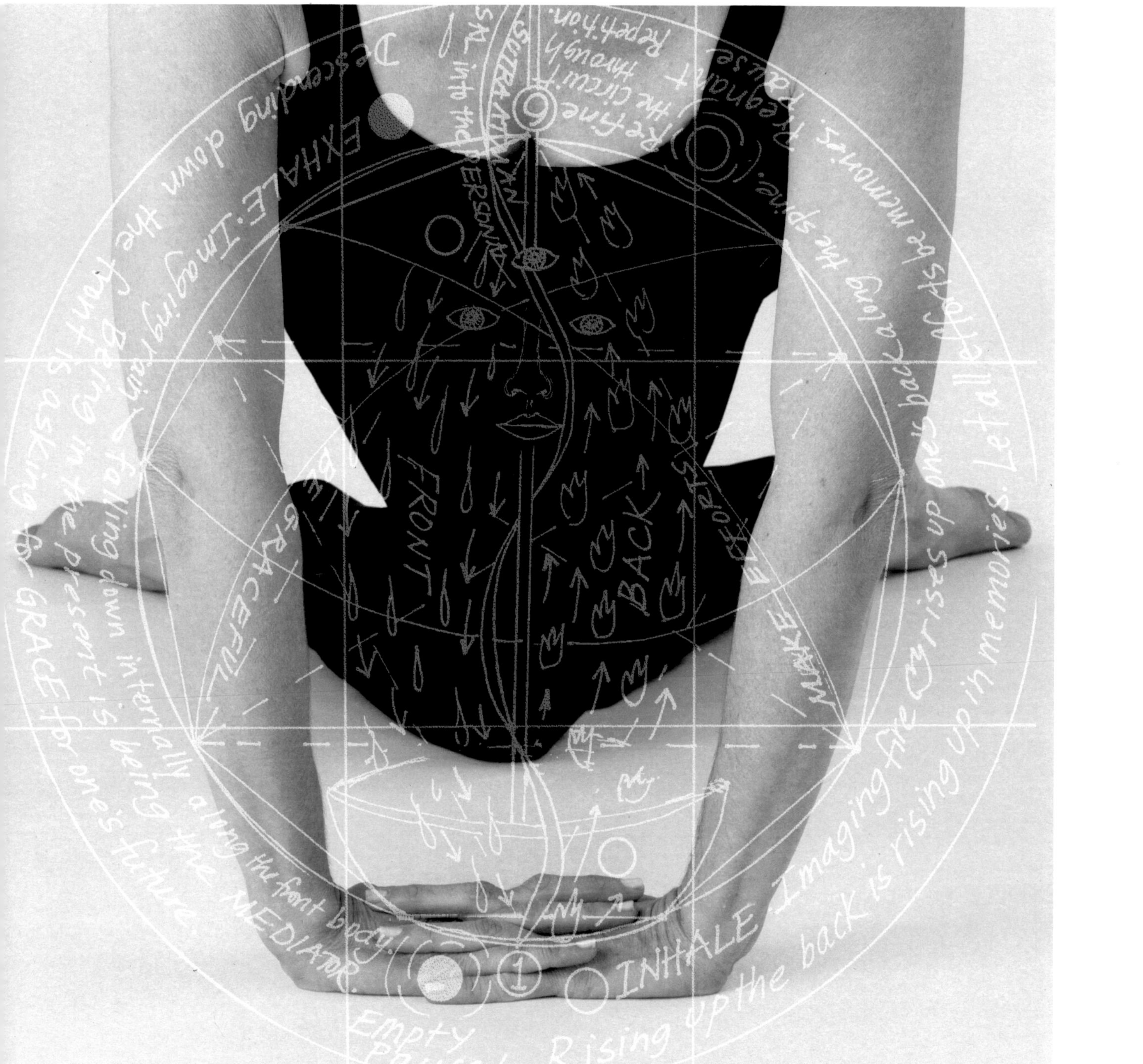

EXHALE. Imagining that being run is being
Descending down the front

being in the present is being
falling down internally along the front body, MEDIATOR

asking for GRACE for one's future.

PERSONAL
INTERPERSONAL
Refine the circuit through repetition.

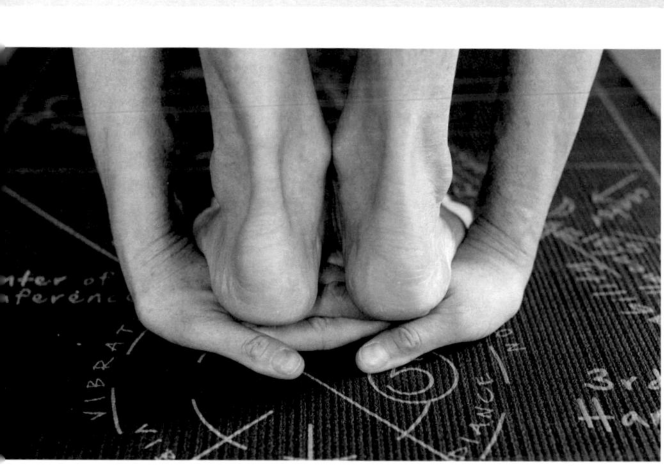

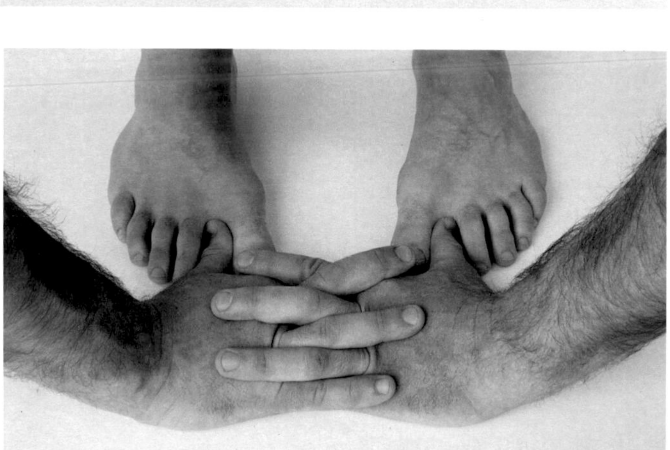

SUSTAIN

FRONT

BACK

BE GRACEFUL

RESTORE

MAKE EFFORT

INHALE. Imaging fire curises up one's back.

Rising up the back is rising up in memories. Let all efforts be memories. Breathing Pause.

Empty
Pause

Rising up the back

center of
ference

VIBRAT

3rd
Ha

SUN SALUTATION

From a Katonah Yoga Teacher Training Class with Nevine Michaan

We are going to jump just in case you aren't hot, and we're going to start with water salutations. You get to pick any piece of music. The goal of this one is that each one of you is a wave in the ocean. Your wave starts in the arch of your foot. It moves to the arch of the knee, the arch of the groin, the arch of your spine, the arch of your neck, the arch of your palette, the arch of your armpit, the arch of your elbow, the arch of your hand.

Basically, this is the idea of the surfer. When the surfer surfs, they don't jump waves. They take one wave and they ride it in. You find the crest and the fall in the wave and you surf it, and your wave is always the wave of your foot because it's designed. You're designed with mechanic proportion and, made bouyant by the wave of the breath, you are designed to fit. You're designed on the wave. This pose, first, teaches you how to ride your wave so you're going to surf your wave on the ten poses. Then, eventually, your wave meets with everybody else so you can build a super wave. The art is to take the personal and move it into the universal. To take the archetype, to take the individual, and move it into the super organism of humanity. That's why one orchestrates and one plays together—to learn that you are all part of the same thing. It is whole and you're going to help each other move through it. [music starts]

So when you're ready. And if you don't know this salutation, don't worry. You're going to pick it up in, like, ten minutes. [laughter] Bring yourself to the front of the mat. Front of the mat. Feet together, palms together. Knees together because it's tadasana. So knees together.

Everyone has enough energy; it's where you put it. Be vigilant in organizing your position. If it's all in your bottom, there probably isn't enough in your head. If it's all in your front, there's probably not enough in your back. Figure it out. You just have to figure it out. It will happen.

Sway back and forth. Every time you're inhaling and exhaling, you get to play gender. Every time you sway back and forth, you get to play time. Every time you orient where you're going, you get to manipulate the direction. Know that, in life, everybody wants to go to the same place—forwards and moving out with their hearts and reflecting with their liver so that you can find their stability in the middle. Everyone wants to feel stable, able and imaginitive.

On an inhale, you rise your arms up. With your arms up, just breathe there for a moment, pull yourself apart, give it some time, and be spacious. These are open and easy. Take another deep breath, bring your palms together. As you exhale, bring yourself all the way down. When you come down, bend your knees, put your palms on the floor, shift your weight forwards, and make your forehead touch your shins. When you inhale, extend your front body forwards, look out in front of you on the floor, make an equilateral triangle with hand, hand, eye. You're looking out. Lunge your right foot back, bend your back knee down, and then find your crescent moon. Bring your arms up. The first variations, I want to play slow because I want everybody really to be on the same page.

Once you're in your crescent moon, things I really want in it. Your front leg is moving forwards into your future, so bend forwards. Your back leg is anchoring you in your memory, so put the weight on the little toe of your back foot or be pumped up on the back leg. Your heart is looking at 2 o'clock, so always let your heart look out. Your liver is always traveling around, reflecting, so always know that your liver travels around memory. And then always see the car in front of you.

Bend deep, bend deep, bend deep. Take another deep breath. Bring the hands down. Pick up the back foot. Bring your front leg back and find your dog pose. And once you're in a dog, give it a moment. Remember that the trick, in all of these, is that every note in music is whole in itself.

Or, rather, every note, will have a character of its own, so a dog pose? You can walk it. You can switch your weight from hand to hand. A dog, really, is very restful because you get a moment to really have enough connection that you don't have to worry about balancing. Take another deep breath whenever you're ready and, now, be a wave in the ocean. So as you inhale, wave your wave forwards so that the last thing that comes up is the head. The heels go back; the head comes up. Now, if you bend your elbows, you can get through your spine even more. That's it. Then, when you exhale, bring it back to a dog. Beautiful. When you inhale, lunge your right foot forwards, bend the back knee down.

To open these, put the palm flat on the floor. The same hand as the front leg. And bend deep, deep, deep, deep in your kneecap. The only way the palm goes flat is when you bend deep enough in the knee and then the knee will know that your foot belongs on its line. So your heel belongs right here. We know you're going to lunge much longer. Feel that? Because if you get the right lunge, now he can use his knee to push his arm and it will open up the heart so that the heat won't be there. Now, you're on the real midline. Beautiful. Pick up the back thigh, take a nice deep breath, and take the back foot and lunge it forwards so it meets the front foot. Then, you fold in half.

Take the hands, put them on the floor. Bend your knees. Remember that the earth is a giant hot griddle. Remember your hands a pancake. Mush down and then push up. Bring it all the way up. Exhale it, bring it back to the heart center, hands together, elbows touching.

There are going to be ten steps. First, we're going to play them slow and then we're going to build them up. Feet together. This is the either going to be done beginning with the tadasana or it's going to be done with legs crossed over. What you're really doing is establishing where the third foot is; it is the eye of the needle. It will thread right through that needle between your legs and between your vision..

Inhale, rise it up. Exhale, bring it down. Inhale, extend the spine out, lunge your left leg back, bend the back knee down. This time, put the kneecap in the armpit. Take the other arm underneath. Hold onto the wrist. Make a nice fist. Don't unbend the front leg as you start to bring your chest up. Your distance was beautiful. Now, if you can, get the elbows all the way up. You stay bending forwards, forwards, forwards, forwards. Exhale, bring the hands down, bring it into a dog. Inhale whenever you're ready and now be that wave in the ocean. And as you wave through, find your fluency.

It is the heels going back. Beautiful, keep coming. Go all the way up, go all the way up, and the heels go back and the heels go back. ♩ Exhale into a dog pose. ⌇ Inhale whenever you're ready, lunge the other foot forwards, bend the back knee down, put the kneecap in the armpit, and, one more time, bring it into a crescent moon that way. ⌇

So, initially, we're just going to break it down one more round and then we'll start really moving. Exhale, bring it all the way down, pick up the back thigh. Now, bring the back foot forwards so you can fold in half. ♩ Once you fold in half, bend your knees if you need to and then bring it all the way up. As you exhale, bring it all back to the heart. ♩

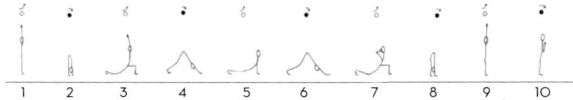

1	2	3	4	5	6	7	8	9	10

There are ten steps. Step one is when you're inhaling. Rise it up. Step two is when you're exhaling. Work it down. ♩ Step three is when you're inhaling. Lunge the leg back, bring the back knee down, bring the hands behind the head and use the hands to hold the baseball just like a great baseball mitt and let the ball come from above you ♩ Exhale, bring the hands down, bring it into a dog. ⌇ Inhale, be a wave in the ocean and move it though. ⌇ Exhale it, move it back. ⌇ Beautiful. Inhale, lunge the foot forwards, put the back knee down, fit the arms behind the head and then we'll leverage it up. ⌇ And that's why every time you change the hand work, you slightly change how you're going to manipulate. Beautiful. Bend deep, deep, deep in the front knee. Deeper in the front knee. That's it. Bring it down, pick up the back thigh, bring the back foot forwards, fold in half. As you exhale, you come back in half. ♩ The breath moves the poses.

The communal empowers the spirit.

Now, we're going to start playing together. We know all the steps, so bring your feet together. Bring your palms together. Sway back and forth. If you know how to do these crossed over, feel free to cross them. If you don't, don't worry; just do parallels. Anytime you're ready now, inhale, rise your way up. Exhale, work your way down. ♩ Inhale, extend your spine out, lunge your leg back, bend the back knee down, find the crescent moon. ⌇ So pretty, Deborah. Exhale, find your dog. ⌇ Inhale, move the wave. Be a wave. ⌇ Find your fluency. Look up. Exhale, bring it back. ⌇ Now, as you inhale, you lunge the foot forwards, you bend the back knee down. ⌇ Exhale, find a hang. ♩ Inhale, rise your way to your highest. ♩

Exhale, walk it back into the center. ♩

So first principle. Every height—inhale—has a depth— exhale. ♩ Every in—inhale ♩—has an out—exhale. ⌇ Every in, find your dawn. ⌇ Then as you out, exhale. ⌇ Inhale then you have an exhale as you come forwards. ⌇ Beautiful. Then you have an inhale, bring the back foot forwards. Then you have an exhale. ♩ Rise it up. ♩ And then you have an inhale. Back into the dawn, ♩ here you can exhale. ♩

Inhale, rise it up. ♩ Exhale, work it down. ♩ Inhale, extend the leg back. ⌇ Exhale, find your dog. ⌇ Now the waves are moving together. Inhale, be a wave. ⌇ Exhale, find your shore. ⌇ Inhale, lunge it forwards. ⌇ Exhale, fold it forwards. ♩ Inhale, ride it high. ♩ Exhale, anchor it deep. ♩

Inhale, rise to one. ♩ Exhale. descend to two. ♩ Inhale, extend to three. ⌇ Exhale, descend to four. ⌇ Inhale, be a wave at five. ⌇ Exhale, find the shore at six. ⌇ Inhale, extend into seven. ⌇ Exhale, fold to eight. ♩ Inhale, rise to nine. ♩ Exhale, bring it to ten. ♩

One is when you're high. ♩ Two is when you're deep. ♩ Three is when you're anchored. ⌇ Four is when you're on land. ⌇ Five is when you're a wave. ⌇ Six is when you're on the shore. ⌇ Seven is the lunge into the future. ⌇ Eight is the fold of the personal. ♩ Nine is the rise to height. ♩ Ten is the anchoring the heart. ♩

It is orchestrated. One is high and two is deep. ♩ And three is back. ⌇ And four is land. ⌇ And five is a wave. ⌇ And six is the shores. ⌇ And seven is the lunge. ⌇ And eight is the fold. ♩ And nine is the rise. ♩ And ten is the heart. ♩

And one is when you arrive. ♩ And two is when you establish. ♩ And three is when you crest. ⌇ And four is when you land. ⌇ And five is when you're a wave. ⌇ And six is when you're the shore. ⌇ And lunge for it. ⌇ And fold for it. ♩ And rise for it. ♩ Anchor and do it again. ♩

And rise to your heights. ♩ And descend to your depth. ♩ After this one, we're going to open it. Right here. You're a wave. ♩ Back into your dog. ⌇ And move it through. ⌇ ⌇ And then you come forwards. ⌇ And then fold forwards. ♩ And rise to the heights. ♩ And descend to the heart. ♩

The whole goal is to move water. That's all it is. That's all I want to do because we're in summer and you have to know, in summer you're building heat. What do you do when there's heat? Find water. If you don't know how to move your water in the heat, you're going to get stuck because water is very heavy. When you're hot and heavy, you can't move. And that's why even when you're doing the same poses, you have to know that you wear the same undergraments but you change the reasons. You change the attitude. You change the colorings.

Yoga is about power. You are powerful when you know. When you know the seasons. When you know time. When you know how to read maps. When you know how to get over yourself. When you get to know your feelings are real but they don't measure up. And when you want to do better than what you think is your best? Get a good tool of measure. It will let you override your feelings. Working with others is partially a tool of measure. Measure up! Play with others. Keep up.

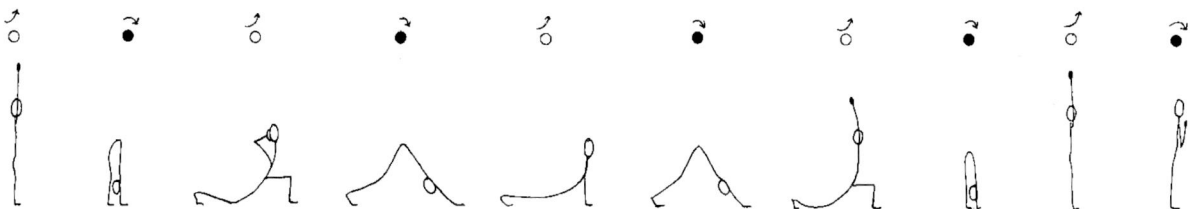

Step 1. Inhale, rise up and salute the sun.

Step 3. Inhale, lunge a foot back, anchor the reflection, rise into a crescent moon; straight or bent back le

Step 5. Inhale, move through an oceanic wave into an upward facing dog.

Step 7. Inhale, lunge a foot forward, rising into the crescent moon.

Step 9. Inhale, rise and salute the sun.

Step 2. Exhale, descend into a forward fold; contact hands on earth, head with legs.

Step 4. Exhale, descend into a downward facing dog pose; position yourself on earth.

Step 6. Exhale, move back through your fluency into a downward facing dog.

Step 8. Exhale, bring your back foot forward into a forward fold.

Step 10. Exhale, find your center.

MOON SALUTATION

From a Katonah Yoga Teacher Training Class with Nevine Michaan

You don't run away from the moon the way you'd run away from the sun. When it gets too hot, you really have to go quickly if it's the sun game. But the moon, by itself, has a certain pull and coolness.

If you don't know the salutation, I'm just going to talk you through it for a minute because we're going to do it to music, too.

One reason to do things to music... I do King of the Mountain to music a lot, for a couple of years, and now I'm starting to do it not to music. But for me it's because music is an easy way to be able to do something that is hard. Like, you have to drive a car for four hours? Put on some good music. So you have to really know, the radio will help. Yogi Bhajan knew immediately to teach everybody to music. That is, in some ways, to play with you. You can keep going because you have a soundtrack. So you can do it to a soundtrack.

The other way to do it is to your breath count because when you count there's a beginning, there's a middle, there's an end, just like music; but the real music will be your breath tracking through connected to the breaths of the planet. But for this one, we're going to put it on music so we can be orchestrated together. Kidneys, which are water—it's all about hearing—and the sound that they really want to hear is the ebb and flow of your breath. Or, the ebb and flow of the ocean.

There are fourteen breath steps in this salutation. Position yourself at the back of the mat. The moon is reflective; we start in the position of reflection and concentration. Start as a seedpod. As teeny-tiny as you can. It's slightly different than a child's pose in that your eyeballs are in your kneecaps and your hands are over your heels so you're so compact that you're a seed. That's where you start because the moon is all about fertility. It's also going to be about moving water—growing—because that's the genius of the moon. Then I'm bringing you back down to become a seed again. So I'm going to pull you through the whole thing, back and forth. If you don't know it, you'll learn it really quickly.

Put yourself in a seed. Inhale and exhale. Take your time, nice and easy. Connect your hearing to your breathing and make yourself very, very compact. Make your breath oceanic; inhaling—the tide coming; exhaling—the tide moving out. As you inhale, 1, start to bring yourself up. Look up and shape the moon. 2, you come forwards and put your forehead on the ground. Make contact with the land. 3, you push through and come into an upward-facing dog. 4, a wave in the ocean—you pull back and come onto the shore coming into a downward-facing dog. 5, you take your right foot forward. Keep the back leg straight—embodying the crescent moon.

So all of this is about really getting yourself in the seed, moving through land and water, starting to see the moon. You bring your hands down, you pick up the back thigh, you bring your back foot forwards and now you've folded yourself in half so that you become a stem. 6, Then, when you're ready, you inhale, you rise all the way up defining the shape the moon in the night sky.

7, Then, following the night sky, you exhale bringing your self down.
8, Inhale, extend your spine out, lunge the right leg back, and now see the moon in its crescent.
9, Then, as you exhale, bring yourself back on land and find your dog. As you inhale, you move through the ocean like a wave and then when you're ready on an exhale, you pull yourself back to the ground so you can then bring yourself back into a seed.

That is the salutation. We're going to move it.
[music begins. Karunash "Return of the Rains"]

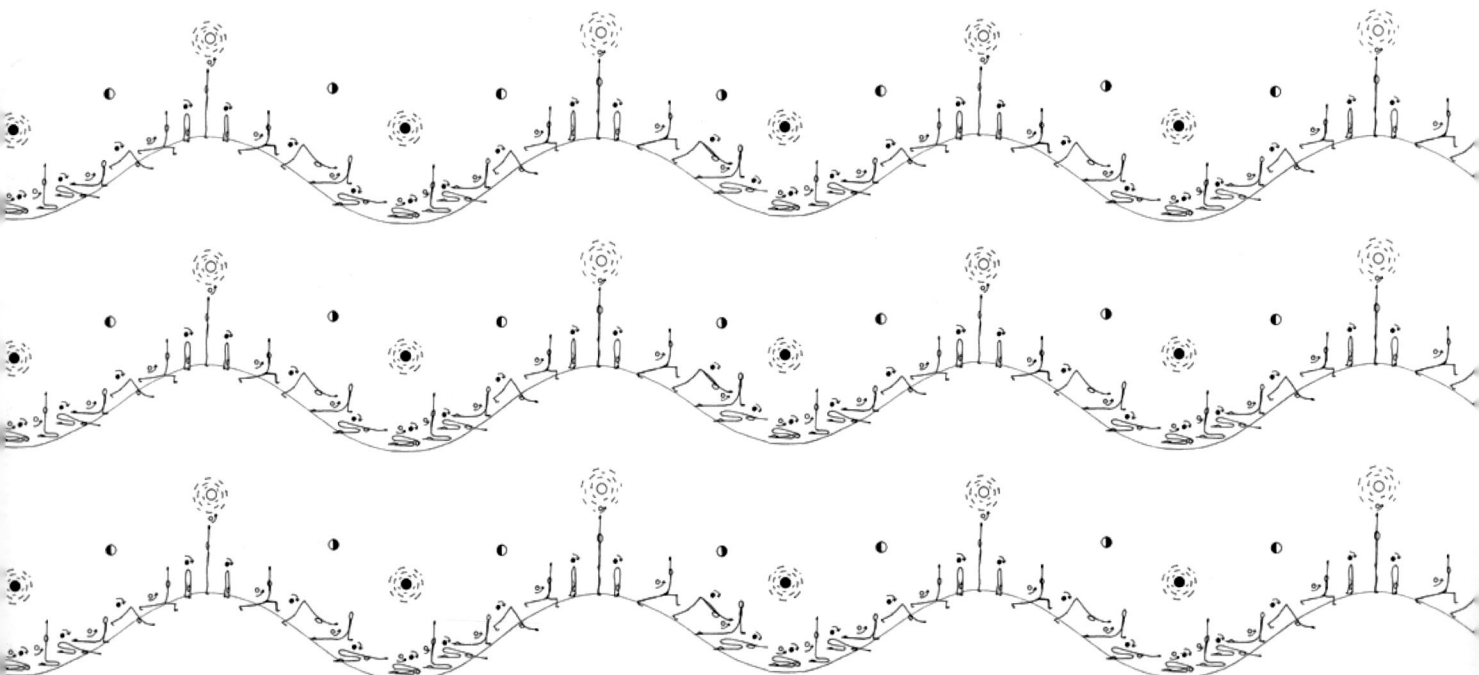

So now, when you're ready, take a nice deep breath, inhale and exhale. The breath in its oceanic nature paces the movement of the practice. When you're ready, inhale 1. Look up. Exhale 2, bring yourself down and then find the land. Inhale 3, push yourself through and be a wave in the ocean. Exhale 4, bring yourself back and find the land on shore. Inhale 5, lunge your foot forwards, keep the back leg straight, and find the moon in its crescent. 6, pick up your back leg, bring the back foot forwards, and fold in half. And now comes the rise so 7, inhale, rise, rise, rise until you see the moon in the night sky. 8, exhale, start to descend again. 9, inhale, extend out, lunge the leg back. 10, exhale, bring it back into its dog. 11, inhale, be a wave in the ocean so pull it through and then, as you exhale, 12, bring it back, knees go down, your forehead finds the ground, and you come back into your seed. 13, take a breath, inhale and 14, exhale.

When you're ready, inhale 1, shape the moon. Exhale 2, find the land. Inhale 3, push through like a wave in the ocean to an upward-dog. Exhale 4, pull yourself back to shore. Inhale 5, lunge the foot forwards and find the moon in its crescent. 6, bring the hands down, pick up the back foot, bring it forwards, fold yourself in half. And now you rise. You rise, you rise and you see the moon in the night sky. Exhale, descend the moon. Inhale, extend it back and you see it in its crescent. Beautiful. Exhale, bring it back on the land in a dog.

Inhale, be a wave in the ocean to pull through and then, when you're ready, exhale, knees go down, butt goes back, forehead hits the ground, and you're back in your seed.

Again, inhale 1 shapes the moon. Exhale 2 finds the land. Inhale 3 moves through the waters. Exhale 4 pulls back to shore. Inhale 5 shapes the crescent. Exhale 6 finds the descent. And 7 is the rise, moon rise, rise, rise, rise. 8 is the descent. 9, the extent. 10, you find shores. 11, find the wave

and then 12, as knees go down, butt goes back, and forehead to knees as you bring it back to your seed.

First principle is, mediate the polarities.

Second principle is, know the patterns. Arch of the foot matches the arch of the groin, arch of the spine, arch of the neck, arch of the palate, arch of the brain. When all the arches are arching in unison, you can surf that wave. So you have to know, why bother? Why bother? Because there's more fluency, there's more joy, there's more integrity, and Great Nature designs it that way.

Third universal principle, principle of repetition. Do things a billion times, you might get an insight. And you might not! But if you don't then do it another billion times until you get your insight. Use the waves and patterns to your advantage Because universe really doesn't care. On the other hand, the universe is incredibly careful. It is never careless. It doesn't care if you get squished by a car, but it is not careless. It gives you ears and eyes and a nose so that you can be careful and not get squeezed. It is your job to use your information. It is about nobody else but you.

That's why you have to know how to be the seed. You have to know how to get pulled by the waters. You have to know how to pull back. You have to know how to see the phases. You have to know how to find the integrity. You have to know how to rise for the moon. You have to know how to descend. You have to know how to extend. You have to know how to find the land. You have to know how to get pulled by the waters. And you have to know how to find the integrity of your seed. Beautiful, almost done.

Inhale shapes the moon. Exhale finds the land. Inhale pulls you through. Remember, everything is a flow. Exhale pushes back. Inhale lunges forward. Exhale, fold it forwards. Inhale, rise, rise, rise, inhale in the sky. [claps] Exhale is the descent. Inhale is the extent. Exhale bring it down. Inhale as you pull through and then the exhale is when the legs go down, the butt goes back, the forehead hits the ground.

As you inhale, you rise. Exhale as you descend. As you inhale, extend. Exhale, you pull back. As you inhale, you know it. So beautiful, people. As you exhale, you fold. As you inhale, you rise, rise, rise. [claps] As you exhale, you descend. As you inhale, you extend. As you exhale, you find the land. As you inhale, bring it through. As you exhale, move it down, butt goes back, head goes down.

If you get tired, you can stop in a wave for a while because the others will move it through. Inhale push through. It doesn't matter; it is waves and waves in the ocean. When all the waves wave in unison, you build a super-wave. You build the oceanic currency.

You inhale, rise! [claps] And then you descend. Inhale, extend it back. Exhale, find the land. Inhale, be a wave. Exhale, be the seed. Beautiful.

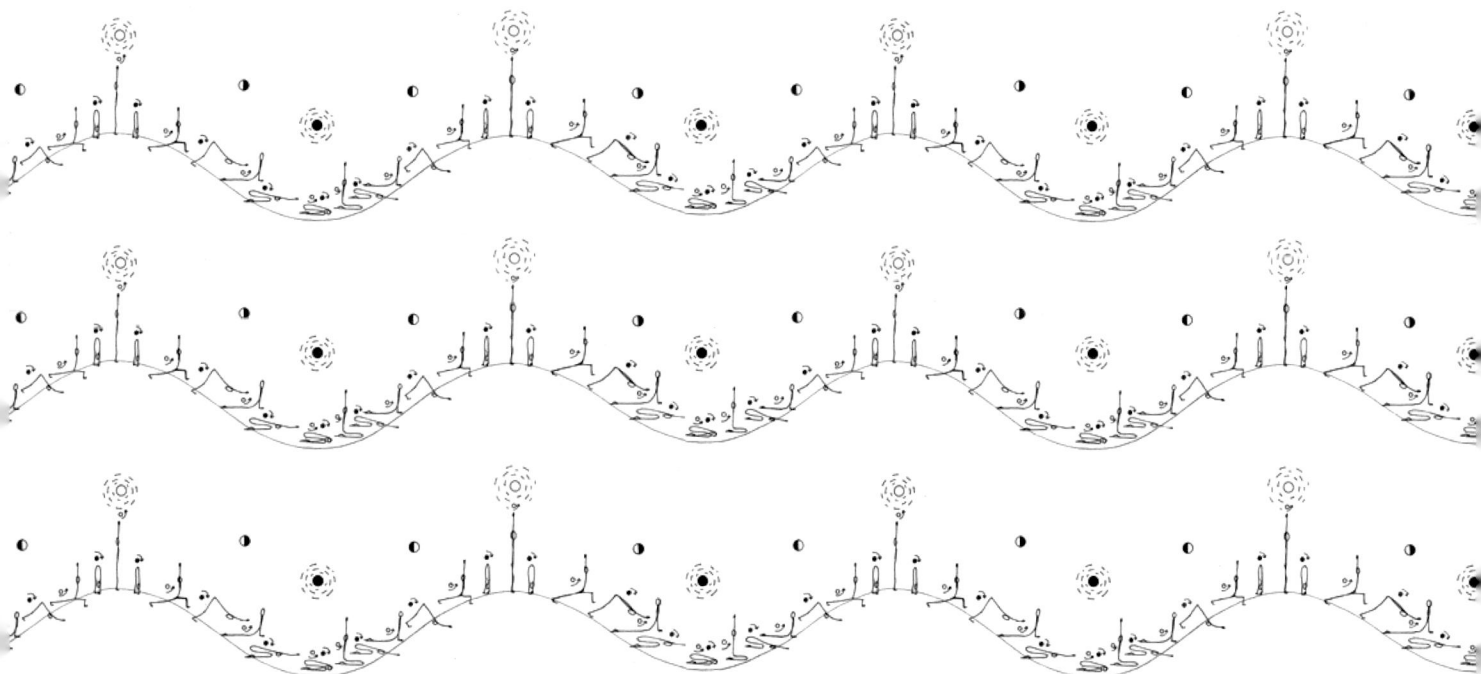

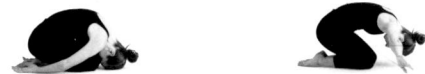

Make yourself into a seed, hands holding heels, eyes with knee caps, inhale and exhale.

Inhale, be a wave in the ocean (upward facing dog).   Exhale, wave back to shore (downward facing dog)

Exhale, fold forwards, be a stem.

Exhale, descend the moon.   Inhale, lunge the other foot forward, embody the crescent moon.

Inhale, get pulled by the wave (upward facing dog).

Inhale, rise the vision, see the moon in the night sky. Exhale, fold forwards, make contact with the land.

Inhale, lunge one foot forward, embody the crescent moon.

Inhale, rise high, see the full moon (the apex of the moon salutation).

Exhale, find the shore (downward facing dog).

Exhale, pull back into a seed. Inhale and exhale, begin again.

The Triumphant Triad: STABLE, ABLE,
SOULFULL NATURE of WATER
EFFORT

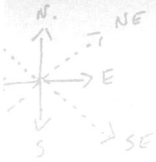

N. NE
E
S SE

any point
can be center

any point can inform a circumference

ge mind

Esote
3rd
Person
Patterns

microcosm of natural world

body 9 obvious portals leading
out of personal
2 eyes   1 mouth
2 ears   1 pubis
2 nostrils 1 anus

develop skillful dialogue by using

ct is the friction th
ialogue. contact i
contact
maintai
external fir
internal

initiates
tes
erates
hemy of
spa
fuel

repeti
forms circu

form informs flow

scious

seeing
smell tasting
touchi
flow/out

dia e betwee   flow

form can be

Mind is the matt
pattern is the

Map- patterned material

pattern is the pater
    Perceval - goal is to pierce the veil of
seperation, loneliness, dis-ease - to
perceive the patterns of the universe
    achieve unity between personal
    and universal

                    to pierce the veil
                        to perceive
                        to be perceptive
                to develop perspective
                to be prescient
develop vision, be perceptive, develop
                perseverence

Veil - vision
    envision
    visionary

Universe always in dialogue - develop conscious
    participation
skillful manipulation of senses by engaging
                            mind

be spherical
think multidimensional
            portal between two spheres
                internal/external through
Ideas as seeds   contact
    inception, nurturing, blossoming, ripening,
decaying.
        understand organic process

dialogue with universal archetypes
birth   elements   building the cathedral
age   nature   building imagination
decay   house   construction/destruction
    emotions   spinning the pot
circulation as informational   cycles in
    refinement through repetition   nature

[right column]

                equidistantly radiant from
            center
Heavenly cycles rolling the wheel of potential
orient self in center of one's sphere
    dialogue with one's circumference
NW   N   NE
                        winter
W   E
                Autumn   spring
    S
                    Summer
    SE   goal setting
    mountain   grace   vision
lake   thunder
earth fire   wind   reflection   potential
            patience   effort   will power
image a heavenly cycle starting at NW
        rolling N.
image a personal cycle starting at SE
    rolling S.   - connect the 2 polarities
                NW ←→ SE

Dialogue sympathetic + autonomic nervous system
    through breath.
        engage form
        orient center & directions
        consciously direct in/out breath
            concentration/radiation
goal for individual to be whole,
    healthy, integrated
    well adjusted, bouyant   oceanic flow

107

As a young girl, dance and gymnastics were my happy place. Movement and being upside down brought me joy. At that age, the play was more interesting to me than technique. My strength was always my flexibility. I knew how to go deep and perform. I completed a master's degree from New York University in movement education, studied at Laban Center for Movement and Dance, and became a certified Bikram Yoga teacher and studio owner. All of these experiences gave me discipline and foundation, but once I discovered the Katonah method I realized that yoga was not a performance, and that I could use my practice to my advantage.

I was fortunate enough to be introduced to Nevine 20 years ago and knew right away I had found my teacher. Nevine opened my world to the link between technical proficiency, insight, and fun. She taught me that being a stretched out rubber band with no elasticity was not very functional. Every Wednesday, consistently for years, Nevine would lead a teacher's practice. She conducted a finely tuned orchestra of yoga teachers in the most amazing way. I was lucky to be a part of it.

I have spent over 10,000 hours refining these poses and the experience has been profound. Learning to map, cross reference, and control my breath has given me the ability to manipulate my emotions, vitalize my organs and glands, and strengthen my bones and muscles. My physical practice is the foundation through which I engage in esoteric dialogue and gain awareness of the worlds within myself and the world around me.

The wisdom that I have received from Nevine and Katonah Yoga throughout the past 20 years has had a great impact on my life. I use my practice to up my function, both on and off the mat. For me, the Katonah material is a way of life. These tools help me find a place of joy within my own mind, body and soul. I am forever grateful to Nevine and the entire Katonah Yoga community for the gift that is this practice and the times we have spent practicing together.

—Melanie Hyman

THE MASTER STAIRCASE

Anywhere the mind goes, the breath can follow.
Anywhere the breath goes, the mind can access.

2017 ©KATONAH YOGA

ATTIC
OFFICE
GARAGE
OBSERVATORY
SHRINE
LIVING ROOM
BOILER ROOM
BEDROOM
KITCHEN
UTILITIES LAUNDRY ROOM
MAINFRAME
WEST WING
EAST WING

Illustrator: Susan Fierro

NEVINE MICHAAN

The magic of the Master Staircase design completes a revolution of traveling a circulating route thru the parts of one's organic construction.

Use the breath to power the imagination to climb, traverse, descend, ascend, access the mainframe and parts of the house the body. The staircase allows the travel to the different levels of one's abode.

The Master Staircase follows the essence of the brilliance of infinite integrity. The sequence, moving from 1 - 9 is the magic.

111

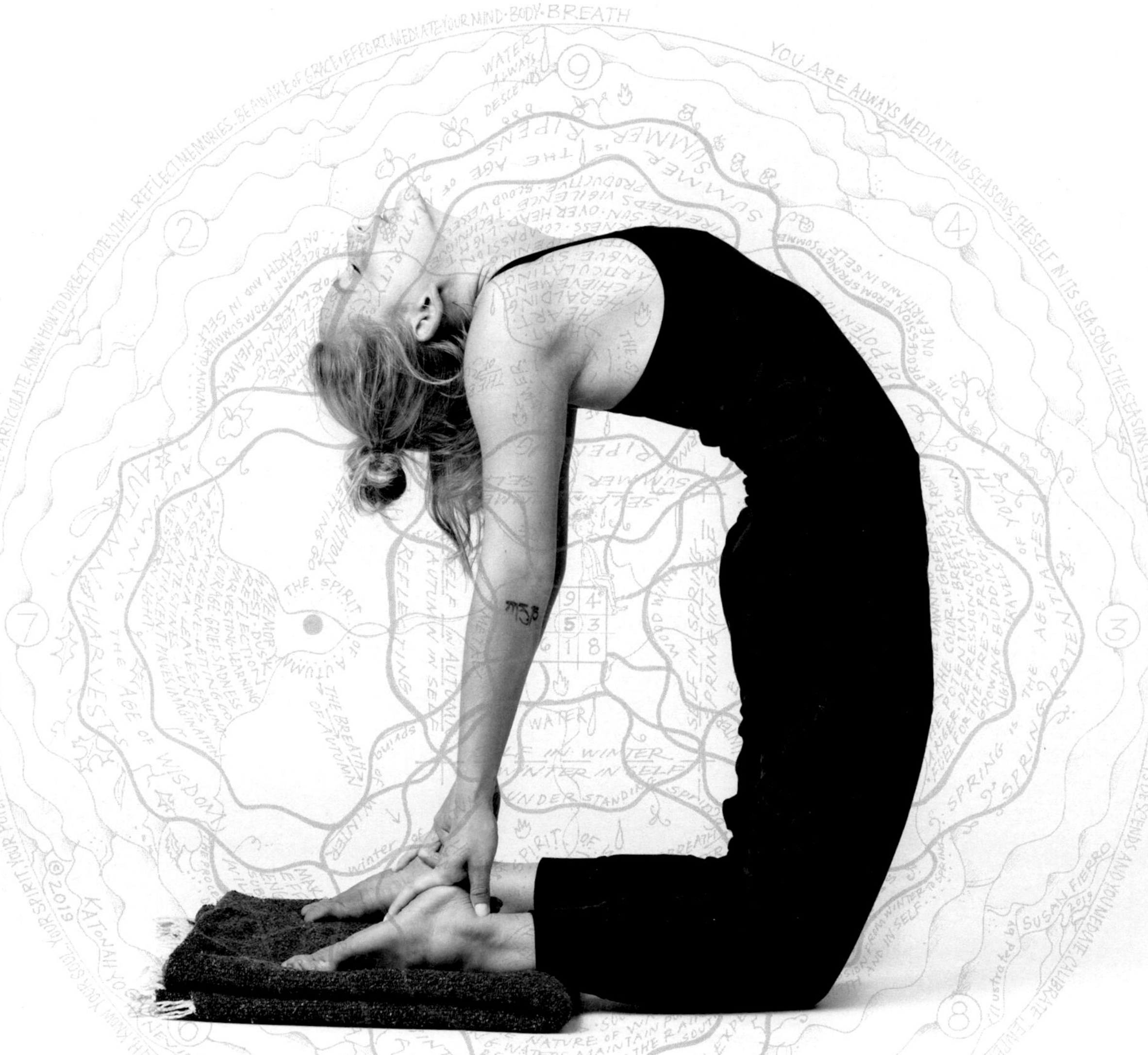

Form, by its very Nature, has certain characters. Form, when not perfect, which it can never be, tends to be deformed, malformed, misinformed. Form can be leaky, diminishing its efficiency. Form has potential to hold information, be re-formable as well as transformable.

The postures of yoga are like origami formulas. I think the goal is to use the archetype of the pose, the ideal, and then descending back into the personal how to use the ideal vision to transform the transformable. Take a piece of paper and make a cup, a plane, a boat... Take a body and make a fish, a bow, a plough... All poses are tools to be manipulated.

The ultimate goal is having facility to use the tools. The goal of a dog pose is not the dog pose, it is the ability through using the pose to achieve strength, stamina, stability. So many ways to play with postures. Straight legs, bent legs are like periods and conjunctions. When you straighten the leg in the dog, you are asking for one adjustment and when you bend, to serve a different purpose. People who always bend should learn to straighten sometimes and people who straighten would be well served to know how to bend.

A sign of good mental health is feeling that one has options, different ways to approach and maneuver around obstacles so, like everything else, life is personal and there is a lot of information in the personal way the individual executes the postures. The skill is to develop more efficient, more refined ways of participating in personal and communal, including familial, planetary, universal well-being.

When I make an origami cup from a square piece of paper, I have in my mind the desire to make a cup that will be functional. I want the pleasure of developing techniques that measure up. When I make an origami cup, I want it to be usable first, then beautiful. Organic materials, like plants, and bodies, are infused by mind and spirit, rather than just material like paper being folded.

The magic is to be the cup, use the cup, and to be used as a cup, oneself being a container for universal spirit, for the breath spirit in spirited containment.

Help form the vessel, hold the vessel, fill the vessel, empty. The body as the holy grail: the cup that holds the elixir of the universe.

GOAL - To create the "float" that can beat the elixir of the universe...

DIRECTIONS to make ORIGAMI BOAT

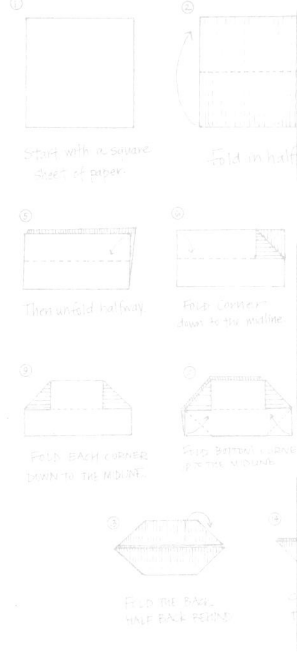

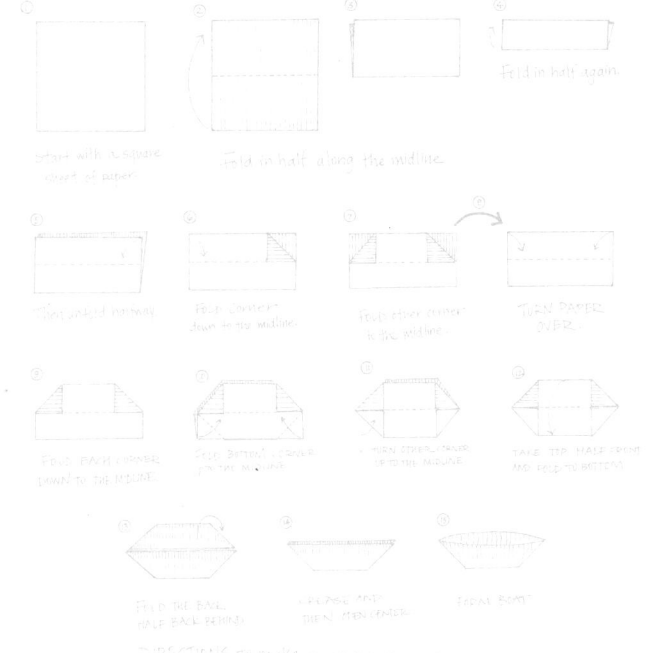

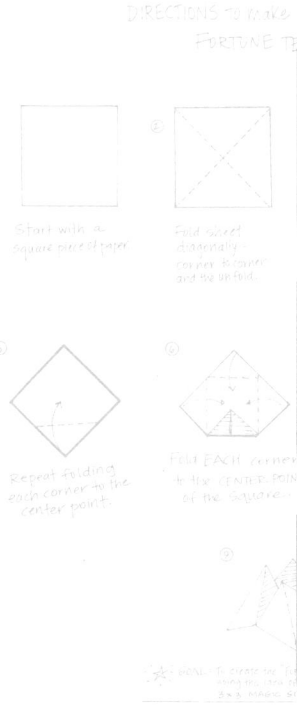

Start with a square sheet of paper.

Fold in half along the midline.

Fold in half again.

Then unfold halfway.

Fold corner down to the midline.

Fold other corner to the midline.

TURN PAPER OVER.

FOLD EACH CORNER DOWN TO THE MIDLINE.

Fold bottom corner to the midline.

Turn corner flaps up to the midline.

Take top make spout and fold to bottom.

FOLD THE BASE HALF BACK BEHIND.

OPEN OUT THEN PRESS FLAT.

FINAL BOAT.

DIRECTIONS to make a MAGIC SQUARE FORTUNE TELLER

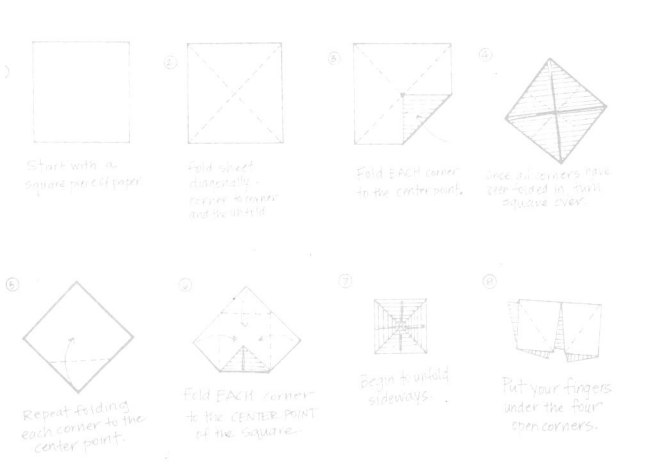

Start with a square piece of paper.

Fold sheet diagonally corner to corner and then unfold.

Fold EACH corner to the center point.

Once all corners have been folded in, turn square over.

Repeat folding each corner to the center point.

Fold EACH corner to the center point of the square.

Begin to unfold sideways.

Put your fingers under the four then corners.

FORTUNE TELLER OPENED.

DIRECTIONS to make FORTUNE TELLER

DIRECTIONS to make a MAGIC SQUARE
FORTUNE TELLER

① Start with a square piece of paper.

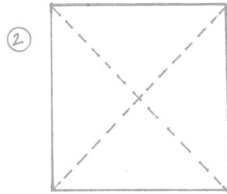

② Fold sheet diagonally - corner to corner and the unfold.

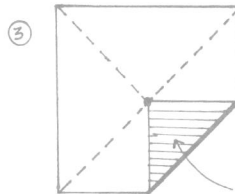

③ Fold EACH corner to the center point.

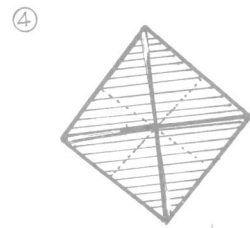

④ Once all corners have been folded in, turn square over.

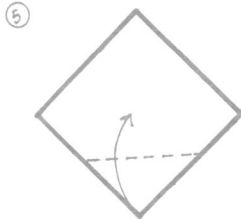

⑤ Repeat folding each corner to the center point.

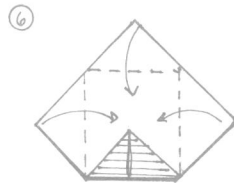

⑥ Fold EACH corner to the CENTER POINT of the Square.

⑦ Begin to unfold sideways.

⑧ Put your fingers under the four open corners.

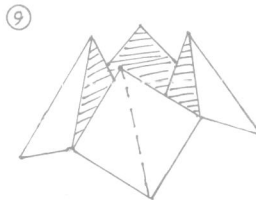

⑨ FORTUNE TELLER OPENED

concentrating

radiating

• wellness • Willingness •
occupy center
Integrated
WHOLE • ROUND • SPHERICAL •

(right) Ab|ove (left)
W ← → E
Below

• wholeness •
mediate polarities
Embodiment

Reaction • Reflection • Memory
GOAL SETTING

Rising the Vision in the Eastern Horizon
VISION of POTENTIAL

VISION

PERCEIVING

②

⑩

④

From WEST to EAST, From EXPERIENCE TO MEMORIES to DAWNING in the HEART

Descent into meditation of the center

⑨

ROUND SOUND

ACOUSTICS

Reflection
TRUST
Fulfill Obligations

ABILITY

raising is vibratory

mediator   meditator
Center of
circumference
of CONCENTRATION

INNOCENCE

③

Uplift

Handling one's feelings
LEFT

Handling
the World
RIGHT

Speech,
the first articulation of feelings
Desires of the Heart

HAPPY WISE

DOING

⑦

⑤

From WEST to EAST

Through tenacity, rise into capacity
Develop skills, handling the world

• OCCUPY CENTER of ONE'S CIRCUMSTANCES •

STABILITY

in the root of the world

⑥

RISK to SUBSTANTIATE
SEX
Establishing one's footing
in the WORLD

PATERNAL ROOT

GROUND of BEING
Descent into ① the personal
THE SOUL IN CONTAINMENT

SAGE THROUGH TIME

techniques to facilitate descent through age

⑧

BEING

AGE
ROOT of
ORGANIC NATURE
Substantiated in Time

MATERNAL ROOT

DEPTH of EMBODMENT

KATONAH YOGA © 2014

by Nevine Michaan © 2014

Traveling Through the Superhighway of the 3×3 Magic Square

(right) (left)
W ← → SE
Below

⑩ · Wholeness
· Willingness mediate polarities
· wellness occupy center Embodiment
Integrated
WHOLE · ROUND · SPHERICAL Rising the Vision in the Eas
Reflection · Memory VISION of POTE
SETTING

② ④
FROM WEST to EAST, From EXPERIENCE Descent into meditation of the center

lection mediator meditator INNOCENC
TRUST
ll Obligations Center of
circumference TO MEMORIES to DAWNING in the HEART ③

⑦ CONCENTRATION
From WEST to EAST ⑤ 3rd Speech,
Hand the first articulation of
Through tenacity, rise into capacity RADIANCE Desires of the
Develop skills, handling the world VIBRATION
Hall of the Whole

Ascending passage through time
Vision in the root of the world GROUND OF BEING
Descent into the Personal
⑥ THE SOUL IN CONTAINMENT ⑧
SUBSTANTIATE AGE
SEX ROOT of
blishing one's footing DEPTH OF EMBODIMENT ORGANIC NATUR
the WORLD Substantiated in Time

PATERNAL ROOT MATERNAL ROOT

GA © 2014 by Nevine M
Fierro

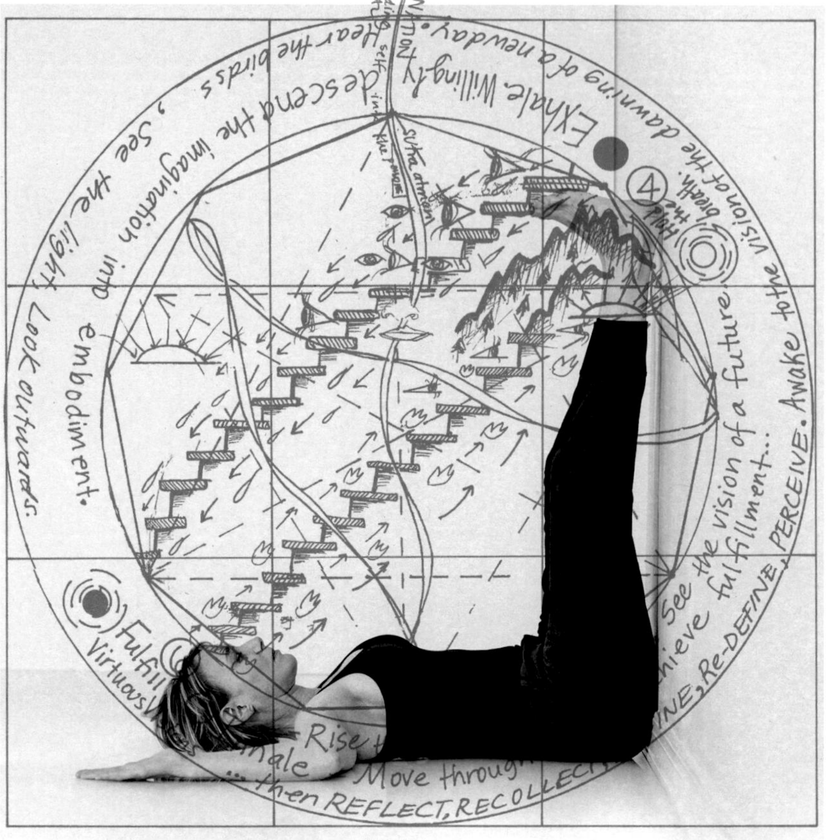

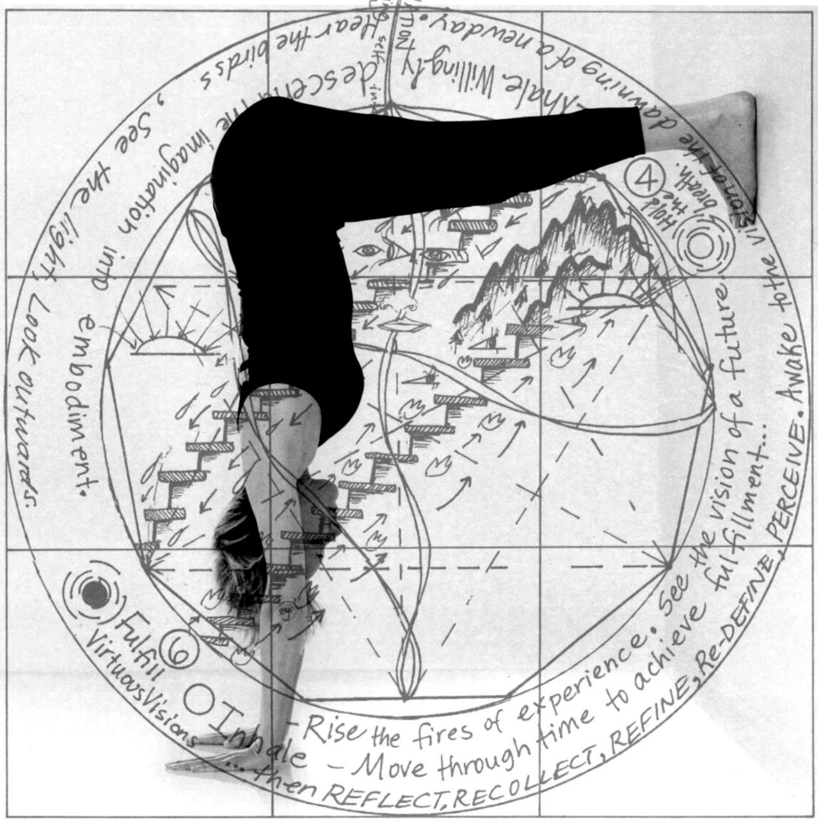

MEDIATED
MEMORIES
behind
POTENTIAL
HANDLES the WORLD
RIGHT
HANDLES the HEART
LEFT
STABILITY
EFFORT
TENACITY

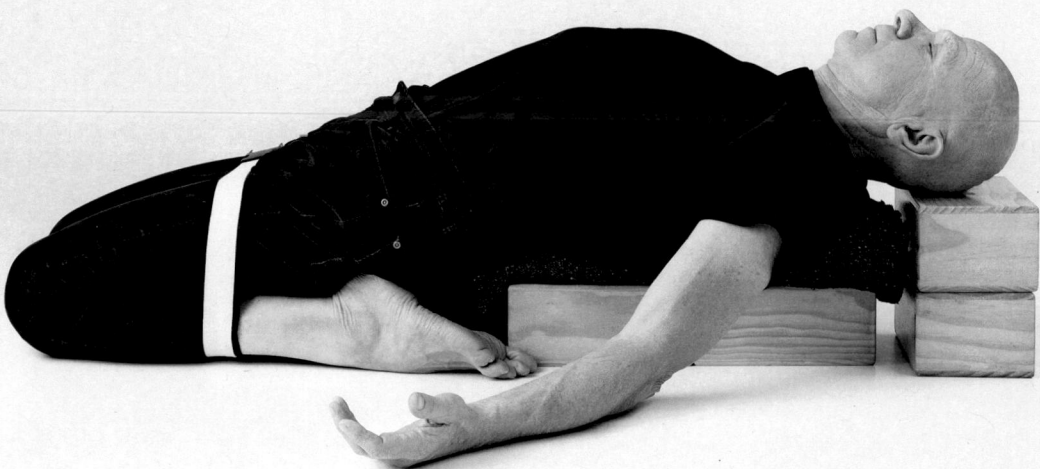

3RD HAND

thymus. Immune

5

BALL is the personal.

4 frames up to IMPLICIT.

reveals the PORTAL to

is center, circumference

Personal spirit

The TRIUMPH of TRINITY

The character of twin

of circumstances

mediating consciousness

potentiated, the personal.

It is one using one's inheritance and one's training to engender Something new. 1 + 1 + 1 is the new product.

CROSS REFERENCE

3

IMPLICIT

5

PLAYER

753

The TRINITY that opens the dimension

produces the BALL

3 distinct strands (potential)

MAGNETISM

INTEGRITY

MUTUAL

Currency of

the third 'available'

Form is formal, functional,
informative, and transformative.

ACKNOWLEDGMENTS

Nevine Michaan and Katonah Yoga
want to give many thanks
to everyone who shaped this book:
photography by Sandra Wong Geroux,
illustrated maps by Susan Fierro,
design by Brian Sisco and Brenda DeRose,
class recordings and transcripts by Sarah Norris,
and our primary model
Melanie Hyman.

Thanks as well to the other models
who gave of their time and talent:
Al Borja, Brenda DeRose, Eva Giorgi,
Alison Grande, Jillian Gumbel, Kent Ishimoto,
Lynn Ivey, Nevine Michaan,
Patrick Montgomery, Harriet Schreger
and Michael Torrant.

Special thanks and love to Steven.

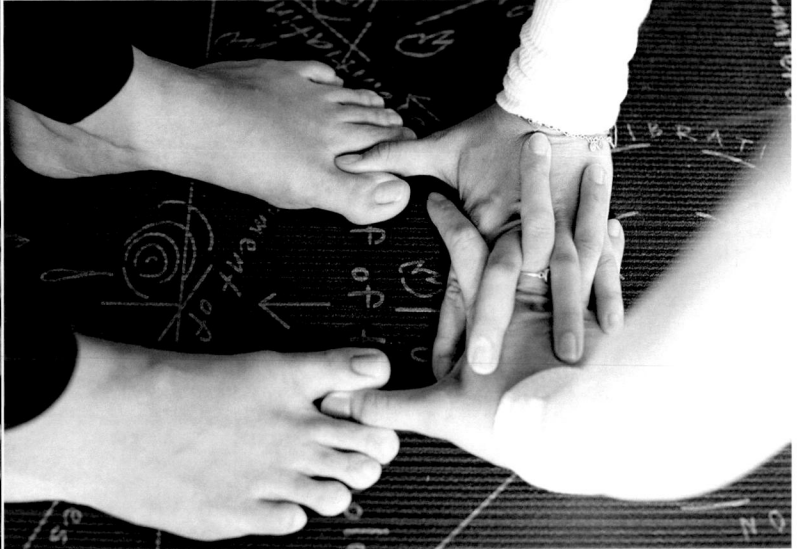

KATONAH YOGA on the mat
Nevine Michaan

Katonah Yoga®
© 2021, Nevine Michaan, Katonah Yoga Center, Inc.
39 Main Street, Bedford Hills, NY 10507
www.katonahyoga.com @katonahyogacenter

Photography: Sandra Wong Geroux
sandrawonggeroux.com

Map illustration: Susan Fierro @susanfierroart

Lighting and digital technician: Ed Cody

Additional photography: Glen Allsop, Maya Moverman

Retouching: Erica Caiche

Graphic and technical design: Brian Sisco and Brenda DeRose,
115 Studios, LLC www.115-studios.com

Content support: Eli Giottlieb, Kate Hansen, Sarah Norris

Printer: Puritan Press, Hollis, New Hampshire
www.puritanpress.com

Library of Congress
Cataloging-in-Publication Data

Michaan, Nevine 2021—
      Katonah Yoga On the Mat
subtitle/Asana
      pages cm
1. Photobook 2. Asana 3. Magic Square
4. Meditation 5. Yoga 6. Maps 7. Salutations 9. Taoism
      I. Title
Library of Congress Control Number: 2021914240
ISBN 978-1-7374491-1-9

This book has been printed in an edition of 4,000.
Manufactured in the United States of America.

For more information about Katonah Yoga maps, charts and theory,
please visit **katonahyoga.com**